A Woman's Guide to the Male Mind

Men's Real Views on Dating, Mating and Sex

BY

SAM GERALDO

authorHOUSE®

AuthorHouse™ UK Ltd.
500 Avebury Boulevard
Central Milton Keynes, MK9 2BE
www.authorhouse.co.uk
Phone: 08001974150

First published by AuthorHouse 1/7/2011

ISBN: 978-1-4567-2210-4 (e)
ISBN: 978-1-4567-2211-1 (sc)

Library of Congress Control Number: 2011900279

Table of Contents

Introduction

In the novel *Breakfast of Champions*, one of the main characters is a science fiction author who writes about an unusual race of aliens. Although the aliens are peaceful and technologically advanced, people keep beating them to a pulp because the aliens' only form of communication is farting and tap dancing. Obviously, this is an allegory for the kinds of misunderstandings that often occur between men and women. When neither gender appreciates the other's history, culture and language, needless conflict ensues – even where farting and tap dancing isn't the cause.

This book, therefore, is my modest attempt to usher in an era of universal understanding and goodwill between the sexes. By helping you ladies understand the male point of view with regard to sex, dating and relationships; I hope to eliminate the senseless conflicts that so often erupt between lovers and would-be lovers. Once you understand a few fundamentals about the male mind and male behaviour, you will stop thinking of men as inscrutable blockheads and primitive misfits. You will no longer regard them as you would a small, nasty child – or an alien race. Arming yourself with the wisdom in this book, you'll increase your odds of finding happiness and harmony in romantic relationships, and you will help ensure that this bliss lasts a lifetime.

Before I move to Chapter 1, please know that most of the advice in this book assumes that you're interacting with *adult* men – men who are reasonably mature and emotionally stable. Though a man's maturity level usually correlates with his age, and most men retain some boyish traits well into adulthood, some men are *never* ready for long-term relationships while others would make great husbands by their late teens.

By the time a man reaches maturity, he has passed through four evolutionary stages in his attitude toward women and relationships. It's very important to understand – and identify – these four stages, because it will save you from wasting time on guys who aren't ready for serious romance. It can also work the other way, saving you from loathsome guys who *are* ready for serious relationships.

The Novelty Stage: This is where junior lands his first girlfriend. This event usually occurs during boyhood, when having a girlfriend is a strange and exciting experience – something to talk about with friends. Depending on the age and personalities of the couple, the relationship may or may not involve sexual experimentation, though kissing is routine. This is where boys learn that girls are actually human.

The Practice Stage: The boy (or young man) knows enough about women and dating etiquette to not make a complete ass of himself, but will still make lots of mistakes. His unconscious goal is learn what makes women tick, gain some sexual experience, and get a sense of what he likes, and does not like, in a woman. These practice runs help him avoid "rookie mistakes" when he eventually meets women with whom he wants more than sex. At this time, he's probably more invested in his friendships with other men than with girlfriends, so he'll dump you if just *one* of his "bros" makes a disparaging remark about you. His relationships with women are based almost entirely on physical attraction.

The Sex Stage: The man's relationships are now based on more than physical attraction, but not *much* more. He wants girlfriends with whom he can actually have a conversation and some fun on dates, but he's mostly interested in getting the "preliminaries" out of the way and having sex. Although he has learned how to attract women, he's not ready to settle down. Now is the time to have fun! Some men skip this phase and run straight to the relationship stage. Conversely, *Players* get stuck in this stage for a *long* time (sometimes forever).

The Relationship Stage: The man is looking to settle down. He knows most of what he'll ever learn about women, and has made most of his mistakes. He's also developed some sexual skills and "special" techniques. Now it's time to find someone he'll be proud to bring home to his parents, and who will make a good wife and mother. During this phase, the man may have any number of romances that don't work out. In between these relationships, he'll sometimes take "Breathers." During the Breathers, he'll pursue one of two options: finding a "rebound girlfriend" with whom to have sex or staying dateless for a while. As men get older, Breathers don't last long, because most men have fewer unattached friends and siblings who will spend time with them.

Spotting the stage that the man is inhabiting will increase your chances of having a fun and satisfying relationship – one that fits your current needs and desires.

As teenagers and young adults, both men and women spend roughly the same number of years passing through the experimental stages. They pick up valuable information about the opposite sex, and rarely inflict permanent emotional damage on each other, despite dramatic break-ups, short-lived reunions, tearful love messages and even the occasional episode of stalking. It's only when the women enter their early- to mid-twenties that most problems start. Here, many women are ready to settle down, while most men are still mired in the Sex Stage. This is where some women (and men) waste valuable time in go-nowhere relationships with the wrong person or continue jumping from one person to the next, searching for an icon of perfection.

I will devote most of the book's focus to *this* critical stage of the dating game.

Chapter 1: Looks *Are* Important

Q: *How can you tell if a man is aroused?*
A: *He's breathing.*

If you remember just one thing from this book, let it be this …

When it comes to sex, modern man is nothing but a Cro-Magnon dressed in 21st century clothing. That's not a value judgment or a joke. It's a simple fact.

Forget all the scientific progress and cultural achievements that have adorned civilization since mammoths and sabre-toothed tigers roamed the streets of London, New York and Sydney. When it comes to sex and attraction, men and women are on "autopilot" – responding to instincts that were written into our genes thousands of years ago. In this respect, nothing has changed since the days of cave paintings and stone axes.

In the ancient hunter-gatherer tribes that roamed the African savannahs, Asian steppes and European forests, men were the hunters and women the gatherers. But men weren't just hunting for bison and bear: they were also hunting for suitable wives. And women weren't just shelling nuts and crushing berries: they were also appraising the health, wealth and personalities of the men they hoped to "gather" as husbands.

No, not much has changed since ancient times, except for one thing – most of us think that because we live in a world of skyscrapers, automobiles and the Internet, the ancient rules of attraction have been tossed out the window. Because we're so technologically savvy, so civilized and so attuned to our feelings, we've convinced ourselves that we're superior to our "primitive" ancestors. This attitude has caused nothing but trouble. It has sparked endless confusion, frustration and arguments as men and women label each other stupid, mean or irrational for behaving in the ways that nature programmed us to behave.

Take the subject of this chapter, for example.

It's a scientific fact that men are attracted to women based mostly on looks. On the other hand, a man's appearance is less important to women. This difference can be traced to our prehistoric ancestors. Scientists know this because: (A) it's convenient to blame dead people for our problems; and (B) there's evidence that men rely on vision more than women, and this dates back to men's traditional roles as hunters.

The average man is *most* attracted to women that are young, beautiful and sport the classic "hourglass figure." Beauty may be in the eye of the beholder, but when it comes to male attraction triggers, *the most beautiful women* share three common traits:

1. They have clear, blemish-free skin.

2. They have a hip-to-waist ratio of 70% – i.e., their waists are 30% smaller in circumference than their hips.

3. They have symmetrical faces.

Note: Both men and women are attracted to symmetrical faces. In other words, they're drawn to faces that, when divided in half, are perfect mirror images.

Scientists believe that these three visual "cues" – good skin, symmetrical faces and the 70% waist-to-hip ratio – helped our male ancestors quickly ID women who were healthy and fertile. They were visual short-cuts for screening potential wives at a time when medical diagnoses were limited to clumsy dancing and incantations.

For those of you who always thought the male obsession with pretty young things was the result of moral weakness or mental defect, my sincere apologies. When a man's head is turned by the curvilinear hips of a fresh-faced 19-year-old, he's responding not out of shallowness, but because she blinded him with science – the science of attraction. He can no more turn off his desire to impregnate her (and assure that our pathetic little species doesn't go extinct) than he can teleport himself to Mars. Believe me, there are many times when men would prefer that they didn't respond according to instinct and biology – especially when certain anatomical parts "rise to the occasion" at the wrong moments.

Personality Can *Trump Looks*

The bad news: Men are initially drawn to beautiful women, no matter how horrid their personalities.

The good news: Beauty means different things to different men. Beyond the feminine ideal that all men find enticing, men as a group are attracted to many types of women. Every facial feature, height, body shape, hair-colour, eye colour and nose length triggers a spontaneous erection and jaw-dropping drool in some man, somewhere.

In addition, most men will overlook a woman's physical imperfections the moment they discover her winning personality. In fact, if a man likes your personality, he'll become *unable* to perceive any physical imperfections – at least for a time. You will become his touchstone for feminine beauty. To him, it will become an objective *fact* that *you* are a stunning specimen of feminine pulchritude. Think of this as a value-added bonus for taking the time to develop a nice personality. Conversely, if a fresh-faced 19-year-old treats men like boot-licking toadies, men will soon perceive her as *literally* unattractive. Their minds will exaggerate small imperfections – and even invent flaws that don't exist – in reaction to her personality.

Before I touch on the personality traits that men find most attractive, let's back up. Let's take a moment to discuss sexiness – a feature that includes *both* a woman's personality and her looks. The dictionary definition of "sexy" is someone who is "interesting or exciting" – someone who "radiates sexuality." Well, that was a big help. Words like "interesting" and "exciting" mean different things to different people, so sexiness could mean anything from swinging your hips as you walk down the street to giving your boyfriend the "bedroom eyes" when you really need to pee.

In reality, sexiness is anything that excites a man's desire. And many times, men can't even put their finger on what makes a woman sexy. One friend claims that a woman he dated in 1989 – for all of three months – is the sexiest woman alive. But when I ask *why* she was so sexy, he can't give me a rational explanation. All he can say are things like, "Her pouting lips and the look in her eyes oozed sexuality. She had a feline way of moving, and her voice would drop an octave whenever she was in the mood. It just drove me *wild*." To me, this sounds like a cat on heat, but it turned *him* on.

My friend *did* say one thing about this girlfriend that made perfect sense. Her personality and those feline movements seemed to reveal a certain confidence.

Confidence is the *one* common thread that all "sexy" women display. Many of the women who've written to me at www.seducemen. co.uk complain that they can't seem to attract male attention. But these ladies notice that some of their friends have *NO* problems here, and that these lady friends have a certain swagger in their step. They often flash a smile when passing a member of the opposite sex, and there's something about their body language that causes men to swarm like flies. That's because men are attracted to women who are self-assured, but not aggressive and competitive. (Men are competitive with each other. They don't need another rival.)

Of course, some women are naturally shy, or lack confidence in their appearance, intelligence, education, sense of humour, etc. These women find it impossible to exude natural confidence, and can't even fake it – unless they take acting classes. If you *were* to take acting classes, however, you might learn a technique that would help you overcome shyness and a lack of confidence.

Designed to help actors get into character, the technique is sometimes called "outside-in." Essentially, the actress dresses like the character she's trying to become. She also adopts the walk, talk and mannerisms of that character, hoping the "outside" traits sink "in." The idea is that the actress learns to *think* like the character by dressing and behaving like the character – learning from the "outside-in."

You can use a scaled-back version of this technique to attract attention. I'm not suggesting that you adopt a new personality. That would be ridiculous, not to mention dishonest. I'm recommending that you make a few modest adjustments to your dress, makeup, hair and body language that will instantly raise your self-confidence, thereby causing more men to notice you. What you do *after* you gain their attention is up to you. If your goal is to raise your sexiness quotient (SQ) from the outside-in, you'll just need to know what men find attractive when it comes to clothing, make-up, etc.

Attractive Clothes, Makeup & Body Language

It's amazing how often seemingly "plain Janes" undergo Cinderella-style metamorphoses once they're placed in the hands of skilled hair stylists, makeup artists and fashionistas. One reason that TV features a never-ending stream of makeover shows is because so many women aren't dressing and styling themselves for maximum male impact. I've *personally* witnessed several amazing makeovers, as have many of my friends. None required expensive new wardrobes or visits to luxury spas. Often, improving your female magnetism is merely a matter of *trying* – actively *trying* to look better. This can involve a new dress, more sparing use of makeup, or a visit to the local salon. At minimum, consult a trusted friend or relative – as long as the person is truly *objective*. Do *not* ask male friends or competitive girlfriends to tell you "what's wrong" with your look. (If a man has any experience with women, he'll run away screaming before giving you an honest opinion of what you need to change.)

How much difference can a minor upgrade make?

How about the difference between a sexless android and a Hollywood starlet?

No, I'm *not* joking.

My American friend Pete recently told me this story.

"When I was in college, I used to hang out in this coffee shop after class with one of my roommates and a girl named Gail. We'd have a few cappuccinos and discounted pastries (after 4:00 p.m.). I never paid much attention to Gail, since she always wore old jeans and baggy sweatshirts. Also, she had horrible coffee breath.

"One Friday night, I was *dying* to see a particular film at a Manhattan theatre. I phoned everyone in my address book, but they'd already made plans. Last on my list was Gail. I don't know how or why I had her phone number, but I called. Turns out she was *very* keen to see the movie. The first thing she said was, "Great! Then we can come back to my place for a bottle of wine."

"I thought, "Sure, whatever.""

"But the minute I spotted Gail outside the theatre, I nearly dropped dead from shock and awe. She was wearing a form-fitting cashmere sweater (lavender), with a black mini-skirt, seamed silk stocking and black pumps. Suddenly, she was a total bombshell – a beautiful young woman with big boobs, shapely legs and a firm butt!

"My heart was pounding, my palms sweating, and I couldn't think of anything to say. I no longer gave a crap about the movie. In fact, I couldn't concentrate on anything but *her* during the show. All I could think was, 'Must touch Gail. Must kiss Gail. Must see naked Gail.' I've never seen such an astounding makeover. The moment I laid eyes on her, I knew two things: (1) I was incredibly attracted to her; and (2) she must like me, because even someone as oblivious as me knew that no woman dresses like that just to hang out with a friend.

"We dated for about four months."

Okay, this example is a bit extreme, but it makes my point. Little things can make a huge difference when it comes to attracting attention. I'm no expert on hair, makeup and clothing, though I know a thing or two about body language. But I *can* tell you the basics of what lures a man and what repels him.

Hair. This is very important, since hair is one of the first things a guy notices – even from a distance. Healthy feminine hair makes him think, "That is *one* attractive babe." He may also deduce that if she takes good care of her hair, she takes good care of the rest of her body.

I sometimes make the mistake of assuming that any woman with gorgeous hair is 18 years old – only to discover that some are as old as my grandmother. *That's* how much difference hair makes to a guy. Whether your hair is short or long, thick or fine, blonde, brunette or red, it should flatter your face – something women tend to forget as they grow older and their faces mature. Too many women – which is to say more than one – adopt a particular hairstyle and then stick with it for life. I know one woman who wore the same style from age 12 to 45, even though she grew 10 inches and gained 80 pounds during that time. (She recently got a new style, which instantly and *dramatically* improved her looks!) Take good care of your hair, and men *will* notice you.

Makeup. Men usually forget that women wear makeup. If you apply makeup sparingly, which is what men prefer, they won't notice that you're wearing it. But they *will* notice your long eyelashes, alluring eyes and the gentle "bloom" upon your cheek. (Blush mimics the flush that occurs when women are sexually aroused.) As a rule, the only time men *will* notice a woman's makeup is when:

- They watch you apply it.

- You've used more blush than a circus clown, and more eyeliner than Cleopatra.

- They ingest huge quantities of makeup while kissing you. Pete once had a girlfriend who wore tons of foundation to cover up her acne. His neighbours learned that whenever they saw her acne, she'd just finished a make-out session.

Use makeup as sparingly as possible – just enough to highlight your charms and mask the little imperfections. Lipstick should be only a shade or two darker than your natural lip colour. Eye shadow should call attention to the depth of your eyes without making it look like you lost a boxing match with Mike Tyson. Eyeliner is designed to *subtly* highlight the size and shape of your eyes, and your eye lashes should *not* look like venomous spiders.

Clothing. Men like women to wear clothing that's age-appropriate and sexy, without crossing the border into slutty. Age-appropriate does *not* mean that all ye who pass age 40 must abandon hope. On the other hand, if you've ever seen an 80-year-old in go-go boots and a mini-skirt, I rest my case. Obviously, there are plenty of fashion options to suit women of all ages, shapes and sizes. The best guide to the kind of clothing that will help *you* attract the "right sort" of man – whatever that means to you – is to follow the advice of trusted experts, friends and family, as well as your own fashion sense. Of course, if you have no fashion sense, you'd better rely on trusted friends, family members and clothiers. If you're showing so much flesh that your date is embarrassed to be seen with you and/or you're propositioned by a dozen old men, you've crossed the line between sexy and slutty. Sexy clothing should accentuate your best features without giving away your intimate secrets.

Body Language. Men are attracted (often unconsciously) to women whose body language conveys interest and availability. However, they are not attracted to signs of sexual aggression, though many men will sleep with a woman who conveys that she wants sex – and wants it now. A woman's interest is often revealed through body language, even though some men, especially younger men, miss subtle signs such as when women twirl their hair and fiddle with their jewellery.

But even the "thickies" will detect your interest if you lightly touch their arms, or your breasts just happen to brush against them.

One of the most common signs of attraction is when a woman begins to mirror the movements and speech patterns of the man. If the man and woman are seated, he might cross his legs and point one foot toward her. She will respond by crossing her legs and pointing one foot toward him. He will lean forward. She will lean forward. His voice will rise with excitement, and so will hers. Although most mirroring is not done deliberately, except by *Players* (see Chapter 4), you can consciously use mirroring, along with eye contact and smiles, to attract a man. You are signalling that you're self-confident enough to betray some attraction to him.

Basic Personality Traits that Men Find Attractive

It's been said that men are *most* attracted to women who remind them of:

- Their mothers.
- Their fathers.
- Their best friends.
- Themselves.
- A talking dog.

It's safe to say that many men are already attracted to themselves – or at least to one of their hands (*both* if they're polygamists). So, depending on the individual, any or all of the above may be true.

It's more accurate to say that men are attracted to women who display a balanced mix of feminine and masculine personality traits. If the woman is too "girly," the man will think he's dealing with an alien life form, and won't know how to interact. If the woman is too "boyish" – just one of the guys – he will unsex her in his mind. She'll become one of the guys.

Most women are subtle about showing interest in a man. After all, if they come across as *too* available, a man will either run away like a scared little boy, or he'll label her a tramp. Thanks to the infamous "double standard" regarding the pursuit of casual sex – expected of men; frowned upon for women – the "slut" label is something most women are careful to avoid. This is why they tend to be subtle when announcing their sexual openness.

Men expect women to be *playful* and flirtatious – albeit not as playful as an Amazon warrior – and they enjoy a certain amount of feminine teasing, especially during the "meet & greet" phase of a relationship. A man likes a woman with a good sense of humour, as long as it doesn't overwhelm *his* sense of humour – to the point where *she's* the last comic standing. When a man is attracted to a woman, he will display his amazing wit and charm, hoping the woman will respond with giggles, laughter and the *occasional* witty comeback. He will *not* be attracted to a woman who tries to "one up" him, since (again) men are *not* attracted to competitors.

A kind and nurturing personality is probably the most important trait sought by the male. This is a huge attraction trigger, and explains why some experts think men are attracted to women who remind them of their mothers. A man interested in more than casual sex is attuned to the maternal cues that a woman offers, including signs of affection toward children, animals and especially *him*. Any woman who listens to a man's problems or lets him rest his head in her lap will score *hundreds* of bonus points. Men *love* to be mothered, as long as the mothering doesn't get creepy and oedipal – i.e., as long as the woman doesn't dress and behave like his *actual* mother.

If you show sincere interest in what a man says, and produce sympathetic sounds (ooohh and aaawww) when he tells you how badly his ex-girlfriend treated him or that his dog just died, you're on the right track. Do *not* feign interest in his career or hobbies if you couldn't care less. Instead, listen attentively, ask a question, and then steer the conversation to a new topic. Asking a question demonstrates that you have a genuine interest in him (if not the topic), whereas saying "That's interesting" might convey that you don't give a crap, which will annoy him. He will know you aren't *that* interested in the topic when you switch the conversation to another track (unless he's a social misfit) but he'll appreciate that you were polite about it.

Men *also* like women who are open and honest. Needless to say, brutal honesty –looking bored or suggesting that he's a world-class dullard – are rarely appreciated.

Men like honesty, not hurtful looks and comments. (Who does?)

By honest and open, I mean that men *truly* hate having to deal with women who play mind games or follow the latest "rules" prescribed by their female friends. Men like spending time with women who speak their minds. They also like women with enough tact to withhold their withering sarcasm and extreme political views until they've gotten to know him better.

In general, men are simple, straightforward creatures who aren't nearly as articulate or talkative as women. The word *laconic*, derived from Laconia – home of the Spartan warriors of ancient Greece (known as strong, silent types) – pretty much describes the conversational style of the average guy. Most men respond best to simple, straightforward conversations, and become bored, confused or even irate when women engage in verbal gymnastics or mind games.

A rare exception to the honesty rule occurs when you want to dance with a man in a nightclub. Extend your hand to indicate that you want to dance, or ask if he would like to dance with you. When he says "no," and most men will, because so few are good dancers, a little gentle pleading usually does the trick – *as long as you tell him that you're not a good dancer yourself.* He will *know* you're lying, because all women are good dancers, right? But he'll also *know* that you won't berate him when he performs clumsy "headless chicken" manoeuvres. He'll realize that you *already* care enough about his fragile ego not to laugh in his face.

This is the hallmark of a kind, nurturing, playful and honest woman. *This* is the kind of lady that most men want to know better.

Chapter 2: Does He Like Me?

Q: *What is a man's idea of foreplay?*
A: *A half hour of begging.*

In addition to begging for sex, there are many universal signs that a man likes you. For one thing, his first attempts at communication will consist of pick-up lines and humour. Men like to impress women with their wicked sense of humour, without realizing that most women detest pick-up lines and male humour. (Do you know *any* women who like Monty Python?) Moreover, he will deliver these pick-up lines and funny anecdotes in a loud and enthusiastic tone – as if he were broadcasting a championship football match in progress. This forced and sometimes awkward delivery indicates that he's a bit nervous about approaching you, and wants to impress you with his clever observations. That's a good thing. If he's too polished and smooth, chances are that he's a *Player* – someone whose hobby is getting women into bed (never a serious relationship).

An important visual cue is when his feet are pointing toward you. This reveals that he is paying close attention to you, and isn't planning to flee within seconds.

An important verbal cue is when he actually remembers something you said 10 minutes ago, especially if he asks you to elaborate on a statement that you made or (blessed miracle) if he asks a follow-up question. As I mentioned in Chapter 1, most men aren't very talkative, so the absence of talking doesn't mean an absence of interest. Instead, men usually reveal interest by *actively* listening. The average man won't waste time in an extended conversation unless he hopes to gain something from it – e.g., some intimate moments with *you*.

(NOTE: These rules do *not* apply in clubs or discos, as loud music and crowd noises make it nearly impossible to hear anything.)

Many men are so poor with words that it's a big achievement to elicit more than two sentences. This is especially true when they're part of a group. However, you may still detect signs of interest even when he's silent. He will look at you, but nervously fiddle with his tie, collar or hands. Instead of speaking, he will react to your comments with exaggerated laughter, particularly if you say something that remotely qualifies as funny. He may also touch his earlobes to signify attentive listening, and thrust out his chest, shoulders and arms to display his masculine physique.

The bolder sorts may even touch your arm or your back whenever they get the chance. Men *rarely* touch women unless they find them attractive. In fact, most men would rather munch on hot coals than touch a woman they find unattractive.

Shy men – and those who aren't instantly attracted to your looks – may not approach you at all. That doesn't necessarily mean "game over." If you're feeling bold and/or aroused, take a chance, and make the first move! Approach *him*. You only have to conduct a brief conversation to determine if things will go anywhere. If he shows signs of interest, he's probably warming to you – even if he wasn't blown away by your physical beauty at first sight. Unless he finds you utterly repulsive, he will probably be flattered that you think *he's* worth talking to. He will gradually move from a defensive posture (folded arms, feet pointed away from you) to an open posture (feet pointed toward you, and hands fiddling with his tie, collar, etc.).

If you're very astute, you might notice that his pupils are dilated, and that he quickly licks his lips, touches his neck and face, and that his eyes travel back and forth between your eyes, hair, lips and boobs. Sometimes, men do their utmost to avoid looking at your boobs, but his brain will force him to take at least a few glimpses. A man who never looks at your boobs is either superhuman or gay. And don't forget to look for mirroring behaviour (see Chapter 1) – another classic cue that a man fancies you.

If a man does *not* fancy you, look for negative body language that includes:

- Covering his face with his hands.
- Tapping or fiddling *violently* with objects (not absentmindedly fiddling with them).
- Playing with his fingernails.
- Glancing over your shoulder at someone else.
- Staring ahead blankly while you talk.
- Short, gruff answers to your questions.
- Feet pointed away from you.

If you are talking with an Alpha Man, you will immediately know whether he's interested – without having to interpret nonverbal signals. Within a short time, he will either ask you out, or abandon the conversation to talk with another woman.

Men Exploit Female Attraction Triggers

Most men are not *consciously* aware of what attracts a woman – what her *instinctive* attraction triggers consist of. But men subconsciously *know* what women want. This knowledge must be built into the primitive part of the male brain, because men complain about female attraction triggers in the same way women complain about male attraction triggers. If women complain that men are shallow because they judge women on their looks, men complain that women are shallow because they judge men by their salaries. Whether a man consciously knows what a woman wants or hasn't a clue, he still competes for female attention based on this innate knowledge.

According to science, the main female attraction triggers are:

- Pre-selection by other women.
- High financial and social status.
- Height.
- Age.
- Intelligence, education and social skills.

If you've ever met a woman – perhaps a girlfriend – who displayed absolutely *zero* interest in a particular gentleman until *you* showed interest, then you understand pre-selection. Women are attracted to men that other women find attractive.

This may seem like a cruel joke of nature, but in fact, it's an ancient *female* shortcut for quickly identifying desirable men. Since the days when men hunted mammoths, women instinctively sought mates with certain physical and personality traits – usually those that would help them survive, produce healthy children, and then raise and protect the children. So women developed a whole battery of unconscious "litmus tests" for what makes a superior man. But testing takes time. On the other hand, if a woman notices other females flocking to a man like pigeons to a bread crumb, she *unconsciously* assumes he's a good catch, since the others have already made the mental calculations for her. He's been pre-selected.

He may as well have the 'Good Husband' seal of approval stamped on his forehead.

Despite the advent of the women's movement in the 1960s, wealthy men remain the choicest cuts of beefcake. A man's financial status and ability to *provide* count for almost as much today as they did 10,000 years ago, though many women no longer need his income or hunting skills. Dozens of studies have shown that women rate economic capacity as one of *the most desirable* traits in a man. Women are twice as likely as men to say that financial resources are important in mate selection.

Short of asking him to hand over his tax returns, how do women figure out whether a man is a good provider? Easy. They look to his social status. It's a reliable cue to his financial well-being. Studies show that high-status men possess more wealth, and provide more food and other perks to their wives and children, than lower status men. This holds true in almost every culture in the world.[1]

Education and intelligence are also big female attraction triggers. An international study of desirable characteristics in a mate revealed that women rank a man's education and intelligence at #5 on the list. This isn't surprising, since intelligence and education usually indicate that a man can acquire material resources – if he doesn't already have them. And it's not hard for a woman to pick up on these cues. She usually can tell whether he's an Einstein or an idiot by listening to him talk for 60 seconds.

Social intelligence is also an important trigger, but it's usually not an obvious feature. It's often demonstrated by what a man does *not* say, especially in situations that require a little finesse. (Kramer on

---

1   Bass, David M. The Evolution of Desire. New York: Basic Books, 2003: 26.

the TV show *Seinfeld* was notorious for his lack of social intelligence.) This trait is key to winning friends and climbing the economic ladder. It's also an indication of a man's emotional stability and talent for connecting with others. The ability to connect with others may also reveal whether the man is capable of committing to a long-term relationship.

A man can demonstrate high value to women by showing that he's a protector of women and children. Women want to know – at the subconscious level – that men can protect the family. After all, protecting women and children isn't limited to physical defence. A man can protect the family from tough times by saving money; he can keep the house from falling apart by fixing things; he can keep the kids out of trouble, etc.

Even though height, strength and age aren't as important as they once were, women still find taller, stronger and older men more desirable. It's programmed into their genetic code! Worldwide, women marry men that are on average 2.5 years older and they prefer taller specimens. This makes perfect sense. Statistics show that taller men are more likely to be hired, promoted and receive pay raises. And older guys are usually more financially stable than younger ones. A guy in his thirties probably has a higher salary and more money saved than someone fresh from the university. Indirectly, age and height are good cues to a man's status and financial prospects.

Although appearance isn't *that* important to women, proper grooming and nice clothes *do* make a difference. Not many women are attracted to sloppily-dressed trolls smelling of B.O. But all you have to do is watch TV or read the newspapers to see that high status, financial success, education and intelligence are *more* important to women. How many trophy wives do you see hanging on the arms of odd-looking rock stars, politicians and businessmen?

Tolerance for Rejection Colours Each Man's Approach

When courting women (for sex *or* relationships), each man's approach is coloured by his tolerance for rejection. This tolerance, in turn, is based on his personality type.

In the Dating Game, men can be classified into five types:

1. Alpha Men
2. Nice Men
3. Nice Guys
4. Players
5. Bad Boys

Obviously, *no* man enjoys rejection. However, each of these personality types possesses a different degree of tolerance for rejection. And the way a man approaches a woman is largely coloured by his personality type's *fear* of rejection. For example:

The **Alpha Man** is a rare bird, comprising no more than 5% of the male population. Brave, confident and assertive, he uses his intelligence to the benefit of others, as well as himself. The Alpha Man is independent and in control of his emotions. In the movies, he is personified by Cary Grant, Clark Gable and George Clooney. Secure in his manhood and with nothing to prove to anyone, he is nearly fearless when it comes to rejection, because he knows there are "plenty of fish in the sea." He knows because he rarely has trouble catching most of those fish.

Nice Men constitute the vast majority of males. While they share some characteristics of the Alpha Man, they lack the self-confidence needed for that label. They have a reasonable fear of rejection – for reasons ranging from a lack of opportunities for meeting "the right sort," to natural shyness, to normal self-consciousness about their desirability in the areas of looks, financial status, social status, intelligence and so forth. If the Nice Man is shy, his signals of interest may be pretty subtle – closely mimicking those of a woman. He may glance frequently in your direction, but avert his gaze whenever you make eye contact. He may appear nervous, botch his sentences, stammer, and seem anxious to flee. He may wait for you to ask *him* out, or force you to make it blindingly obvious that you're interested, especially if he's young. (Young men often have *no* clue when a woman is interested unless she comes out and says so.)

Many women mistake **Nice Guys** for Nice Men – at first. There are many superficial similarities between the two, with the key difference being that Nice Guys have little or no self-esteem. In fact, the Nice Guy's self-esteem is located at such Stygian depths that he's basically a living doormat. He is so desperate to worm his way into your good graces that he will submit to any indignity, erase any independent thoughts or actions from his brain, and follow you around like a homeless puppy in the hope that you will eventually see what a "nice guy" he is, and abandon the brutish Neanderthals you normally date.

His agenda is simple-minded and single-minded – to win your undying love by becoming your best buddy. This type is so paralyzed with the fear of rejection that he will *NEVER* ask you for a date. Instead, he will become your loyal lackey, secretly plotting and planning for the day when one of your boyfriends breaks your heart. On that day, *he* will be there to pick up the pieces and assemble them into his own graven image. He probably won't make his move until that day – when you are crying your eyes out over a shattered romance – at which point he will start to clumsily grope you. If you've ever seen *Lord of the Rings*, you'll easily recognize this character as Gollum.

Many men behave like Nice Guys at some point in their lives. Do yourself, and them, a huge favour. In a kind and gentle tone, tell them to "Piss off and man up!"

The Player. See Chapter 4. For now, simply note that women should avoid Players like the bubonic plague, unless you are keen for a one-night stand.

The Bad Boy is often mistaken for the Alpha Man, because he is the Alpha Man's evil twin – the dark side of the same masculine force. Unlike the Alpha Man, the Bad Boy confuses assertiveness with aggression, confidence with cockiness, and charm with the behaviour of a rutting pig. This type frequently surrounds himself with loyal subordinates in order to provide the necessary confidence and goading (alcohol also helps) to approach an unknown woman. This group support also serves as a failsafe mechanism in the event he's rejected, as he will then return to his comrades with a shrug and a smirk, suggesting that his target was a bitch or a lesbian.

Depending on the man's personality type, and since men all know (at some level) what women find attractive, most guys will eventually say something about their career and financial status. Even if the man admits that he doesn't have two pennies to rub together, this – at least – constitutes an admission that he knows money is important, and he's planning to remedy the situation. A man who finds you attractive will also:

➢ Make attempts to display his wit, intelligence and education (if he has one).

➢ Ask lots of questions and/or display a keen interest in learning more about you.

➢ Demonstrate his social skills by not making a fool of himself, or by entering the scene with a group of loyal friends and co-workers. The latter demonstrates that he is capable of maintaining relationships with other human beings, or in the case of some personality types, that he is a leader of men, which also speak to his social status.

How Men Respond to Rejection

When you reject a man, he will usually react in one of the following ways:

- ✓ He will pretend you no longer exist by refusing to even make eye contact.

- ✓ He will make it known that he's found another woman, implying that you've missed your one and only chance for ever-lasting bliss.

- ✓ He will indicate that he was *never* really attracted to you – after which, he may recite a list of your shortcomings to support this argument.

- ✓ He will go quiet for a while, and may excuse himself to the bathroom. Minutes later, he will reappear and treat you like a good friend. This usually happens when he's known you for a while, and can't summon the anger to end the relationship and treat you like rubbish. Make no mistake: he will be hurt and embarrassed, and will behave awkwardly – if only for a little while.

- ✓ He will choose one of the tactics above AND spread malicious rumours.

Chapter 3: Flirting Will Get You *Anywhere*

A woman's definition of a successful date varies with her age:

17: Burger King.

25: Free meal.

35: A diamond.

48: A bigger diamond.

65: Home alone.

One of the most frequently asked questions at www.seducemen.co.uk is: *"Am I coming on too strong with a man?"* Many women aren't sure where to draw the line between showing interest and scaring the pants off some poor fellow (not literally) with a ceaseless barrage of amorous signals.

On this question, here's all you need to know …

If a man finds you attractive, it's nearly impossible to "come on too strong," provided you are emotionally stable. Conversely, if a man finds you as repulsive as a giant slug, *anything* you do will be seen as "coming on too strong." He will recoil from your advances and be gone from your sight as soon as possible.

One of my friends used to spend 45 minutes in a pub before heading to a nearby university, where he was taking voiceover lessons (learning to narrate radio and TV advertisements). One classmate was an older, heavier woman with whom he enjoyed talking before class. Well, he enjoyed chatting with her until the evening that she opened the discussion by remarking on his "delicious young body," and suggesting they go back to her place for a roll in the hay. Fortunately (for my friend), only one class remained in the semester, because he quickly excused himself to the restroom, and never went to another class (or that pub) again.

If a man isn't attracted to you, any romantic overture will be an unwelcome advance. This is an inconvenient truth if ever there was one.

If he *does* like you, you'd have to convey hyper-aggressive or deranged behaviour to scare him away.

A major exception to the rule is whenever alcoholic beverages are consumed during the initial meeting. Many of the letters I receive concern "romances" that started off well, but ended soon afterward – when the man inexplicably refused to return phone calls, emails and texts. In many of these cases, the object of the woman's affection was wearing "beer goggles" at their first meeting.

Mystery solved.

If you've ever gone to a party, a pub or a club to meet someone new, you're familiar with beer goggles. In addition to reducing your inhibitions, alcohol has the peculiar effect of making men and women appear more attractive than they would normally seem. At one time or another, the combination of reduced inhibitions and looser attraction standards causes almost every man to woo a woman he'd normally avoid. Needless to say, more than one couple has woken up the next morning, only to think, "Oh … My … God, *why* am I in bed with [him/her]?"

In sober circumstances, "coming on too strong" usually occurs immediately before or after the first date, and consists of the following female behaviours:

- Phoning, emailing or text-messaging him 15+ times per day.

- Becoming possessive, jealous or needy – in some cases, performing scene-by-scene remakes of the movie *Fatal Attraction.*

- Treating the relationship as if it's existed for 20 years – e.g., inviting him to spend next weekend at your parents' house, suggesting you shop for new wallpaper and furniture for his place, talking about marriage and children, etc.

- Displaying over-the-top sexual aggression and/or sexual preferences – e.g., pawing at his private parts, pushing him to have sex in public places, producing ball gags and leather masks from your closet, suggesting a three-way with your ex-boyfriend, etc.

The Perils of "Frustration Attraction"

Truth be told, women are rarely *too* aggressive when it comes to making their desires known, provided the men find them attractive. Most initial communication problems stem from playing "too easy to get" or "too hard to get." Very few men are attracted to women who take either of these routes. Instead, men prefer that women walk the line between these extremes.

Every self-appointed love guru who's published a manual on how to attract men claims that frustration attraction is the secret "key" to winning a man's affection, and will prompt him to pursue a serious relationship. This is pure rubbish.

Frustration attraction is generated in human beings when they encounter an obstacle to winning the affections of their "love interest." *Romeo and Juliet* is a case history in frustration attraction. The harder the Montagues and Capulets tried to keep these star-struck teenagers from being a couple, the more the would-be lovers obsessed over getting together. That's *exactly* how frustration attraction works in the real world.

Obstacles and challenges to attaining your dream lover (or any desirable goal) trigger dopamine production in your brain – the "feel good" chemical that's released when people exercise, experience joy, or imbibe substances like alcohol. Dopamine is also produced when a goal seems just out of reach.

But Dopamine is a double-edged sword. Although it makes you feel good, it also causes you to become more persistent, focused and even *obsessive* when it's withdrawn. If a woman plays *too* hard to get – i.e., moves the goal post from "within reach" to "nearly impossible," she *may* cause a man to become *obsessed*. This, in turn, might cause anger, rage, and even violence, depending on the man's personality.

While a little frustration attraction *can* turn a lukewarm suitor into a love-crazed Casanova, too much frustration attraction can turn a man into a stalker or a psychopath. The last scenario isn't very common, so I wouldn't bar the door and windows just yet. Nor would I jump into bed with every man who says "hi' to avoid being stalked. Just be careful not to go overboard.

Keep in mind that playing "hard to get" is *not* a male attraction trigger. It's the exact opposite. A man must *already* find you desirable for frustration attraction to kick in. That's because playing "hard to get" is a signal of *disinterest*.

How many men continue to pursue women whose words and deeds convey the message, "Piss off!" Answer: not many. Unless you're a remarkably physical beauty, playing "hard to get" backfires *much* more often than it succeeds. Believing that you have no interest in them, most men will seek out greener pastures instead of continuing to pursue you.

A modest amount of frustration attraction reveals that you aren't about to jump in bed with a man in the next 60 minutes – that you want to build a relationship before having sex. Most men understand this point of view, and will appreciate the small obstacles you place before them. Most men will *not* appreciate an Olympic-level challenge in which only "gifted athletes" (extraordinarily handsome or wealthy men) can finish the race. Be sure your challenges are achievable for the man in question.

By definition, being "too easy" means that you're not setting boundaries. If you aggressively flirt or have sex with almost any guy, you will turn off the men who are looking for a challenge/ serious relationship, and *attract* the guys whose *only* interest is sex. You are also telling the world that you have low self worth and low standards.

Yes, this is a double standard, since people rarely criticize men for having low standards or being "sluts." Unfortunately, this is how the world works. Men are expected to "play the field" because they are programmed to have sex with almost every eligible and nubile woman. Women are expected (to some degree) to be selective about *when* they'll have sex and with *whom*.

Male Rules on Flirting

If a guy initially shows interest, but disappears after "first contact," odds are high that either you played "too hard to get" or "too easy to get" (especially if you had sex with him immediately before/after the first official date). Men love to flirt almost as much as women, but they can be easily turned off. They tend to follow certain rules of flirting, and any woman who violates the rules may find herself abandoned on a barstool, wondering if/when her suitor will return from the toilet.

Men enjoy being teased by women, but not physically or mentally abused. Who does? To follow are two examples of female teasing – one good, one bad.

<u>Good</u>

HIM:	*I don't mean to brag, but I mopped up the field with the other team that afternoon, almost single-handedly.*
HER:	*Oh my. I certainly hope your prowess on the football field translates into off-the-field activities. [giggles].*

<u>Bad</u>

HIM:	*I don't mean to brag, but I mopped up the field with the other team that afternoon, almost single-handedly.*
HER:	[Punches his arm with enough force to penetrate steel.] *You don't look that tough to me. I'll bet you play football like a 10-year-old girl.*

In the first example, the woman massages the man's ego by affirming his athletic prowess through subtle sexual teasing (and innuendo). In the second, the woman crushes several blood vessels in the man's arm, and emotionally emasculates him. She was probably trying to be just "one of the boys." Regardless of whether she succeeded, the man is now physically and emotionally hurt, but will probably not reveal this fact.

Again, men like women with a sense of humour, but not when that sense of humour overshadows their own. In addition, most men like to test certain boundaries, especially when it comes to making women jealous. In 99% of these instances, the man hopes to provoke a playfully jealous reaction from the woman – as when she "catches" him gawking at another female. Consciously or unconsciously, he hopes that she'll reproach him in a humorous, ego-fuelling manner, saying something like, "Easy there, stud. Keep your eyes on *this* prize before you decide to win a Guinness Record for the most women conquered."

Notice that the woman has inflated his sense of self-worth by suggesting he's capable of attracting enough women to win a prize, and demanding that he prove his newfound loyalty by not staring at other women. Men absolutely *love* this kind of teasing!

What men *hate* is teasing that pushes their "insecurity buttons." These buttons usually involve teasing him about female attraction triggers – or perceived female attraction triggers. The list includes, but is not limited to:

> ➢ Jokes about his penis size.
> ➢ Jokes about his appearance.
> ➢ Implying that he's a mama's boy.
> ➢ Demeaning his intelligence.
> ➢ Demeaning his career choice.
> ➢ Demeaning his financial status.
> ➢ Demeaning his height.
> ➢ Demeaning his social skills.

> ➤ Daring to *ever* question and/or make light of his sexual prowess!

Keep your touching subtle at first. If you want to reveal interest, touch his body in non-erotic zones such as the shoulders, arms and hands. Whenever you're in his car or the back of a taxi, be cautious about kissing. Passionate kissing may lead to straying hands if he becomes excited and decides to "get down to business" in the car. If you're ready for passionate kissing, do this while you're on the date. Confine public displays of affection to a peck on the cheek or lips when you're in restaurants, theatres, etc. Do *not* believe any excuse he makes to enter your home "for just a minute."

You must make a guy feel good before he'll be willing to reciprocate. Convince him that you won't hurt his feelings *and* hint that he stands a good chance of winning your affection. If you ignore him or belittle him, he will never warm to you.

Make him think he's in control of the conversation (and the relationship).

Make him think he's the greatest thing since the personal computer.

Make him believe he's the centre of your universe, and you will become the centre of his universe – at least for a time.

Tips to Keep You Sane

> ➤ **Don't analyze his every word.** Men often speak without thinking – much. They sometimes text and email without thinking, though they're usually better at written communications than verbal ones. If you analyze his every word for signs that you have won his favour, or fallen from grace, you will drive yourself nuts. If you simply must analyze his every word, hire an unemployed Kremlinologist to

help you decipher the clues – you know, the ex-intelligence analysts whose job it was to advise presidents and prime ministers on whether the current Soviet Premier was dying, based on the colour hat his successor was wearing at the latest May Day parade. You'll still drive yourself nuts, but now you'll have company.

➤ **Never assume that you're not attractive, young enough or smart enough for him.** There's at least *one* man for every woman, and probably lots more. Low self-confidence is not sexy. If you believe that you're not attractive, young or smart enough to attract a man, then take a college class or get a makeover. (See Chapter 1.)

➤ **Men only claim to prefer blondes.** Believe it or not, not all men are super-attracted to blondes. My friend Pete goes mental over women with long *black* hair. Many men *think* they prefer blondes, because this hue is so distinctive, and once upon a time there were so few blondes worldwide that these women were considered rare and precious delicacies. That said, *natural* blondes have one key advantage over other women. They possess more hair follicles than people with other hair colours. It's true! (Redheads have the fewest follicles.) As long as a woman takes care of her naturally blonde hair, she'll turn heads. I have a rule: *All blondes look good from the back.* Time after time, my head pivots whenever I spy a long and lustrous mane of blonde hair. But more often than not, closer inspection reveals that she's my grandmother's age or isn't all that attractive.

➤ **Men will notice other women.** Men will notice other women, even when they only have eyes for you. They can't help themselves. It's been programmed into their DNA to hunt for nubile females and evaluate their worth as potential mates. Feel free to tease or gently chastise him about his lustful stares and clumsy flirtations, but don't be alarmed – unless he begins ignoring you, making excuses to leave your presence and/or fails to return texts, phone calls and emails.

When a man decides to pursue someone else, you'll receive little or no warning – unless you're already in a long-term relationship.

➢　　**Most men fantasize about other women, but will be faithful to you.** What I've said also applies to the male fantasy life. No need to worry unless he gives some indication that he's about to act on the fantasies. And by that point, he probably has.

Chapter 4: Do You Attract
the Wrong Type?

Q: *Where do you find a man who's truly into commitment?*
A: *A mental hospital.*

I'm often asked, *Can bad boys become good?*

My standard answer: *Anything is possible, but it's unlikely.*

The odds that a bad boy will reform are as likely as being hit by a meteor weighing precisely 1.789 metric tons. Men rarely change much after reaching 16 or 17 years of age. They *do* learn as they progress into adulthood, but this learning tends to reinforce whatever traits they already had.

Many women harbour a common pre-conception of what makes a good man. In reality, these "good man" features have never been combined in any living male. Men are essentially grown up boys, so whatever forces shaped their characters and personalities in childhood have already made an indelible stamp. The lesson: attempting to reform a bad boy is a futile exercise. In fact, attempting to change *any* man is usually a self-defeating task.

If you are consistently attracted to (or attract) the wrong kind of man, you're better off trying to change your own tastes, or "recalibrating" the signals that you keep sending out that attracts these losers.

Here's another inconvenient truth. People can only change themselves, and this usually requires outside help and enormous willpower. No surprise, then, that women *rarely* make even small dents in men's ingrained habits and character flaws. What women *usually* succeed in doing is annoying men with non-stop nagging about how badly they need to change. Nagging breeds resentment, and in 95% of cases, the man will simply take his bad habits "underground" and pretend that he's changed. If you've ever seen the show *King of Queens*, please note that this is not a sitcom, but a documentary about an actual married couple – at least it should be.

Men do not like to lie.

Men do not like to change.

Given a choice between the two, men will lie *every time*.

Why Married Men and Bosses Are Attractive

Men who are already spoken for, especially married men, are very attractive to women. Fortunately, most women have the good sense not to become involved with married men, because clichés such as "he will never leave his wife" are usually true.

Bosses are attractive to women, but most women have the good sense not to become involved with their bosses, because the cliché about losing your job or being stuck in a hostile work environment if the relationship doesn't work out is also true.

My advice: Do *not* get involved with your boss or a married man, especially if he's the same person.

The reason many women are attracted to married men and bosses is because they exude more *self-confidence* than most single men, regardless of what the guy was like before getting married or assuming a position of authority in the company.

Self-confidence is sexy.

What's more, married men have nothing to lose by flirting, since they usually don't expect anything to happen. And even when they hope something *will* happen, a few rejections (or even a few hundred) won't inflict as much damage to his ego as they did when he was single. He already *has* a woman. He's already proven to himself that *someone* on the planet finds him desirable. Therefore, if you don't find his personality magnetic and his body irresistible, then something is wrong with *you*.

These days, your boss is less likely to overtly flirt – or ask you on a date – whether or not he's married. Today's laws about sexual harassment have helped to defeat this problem – or opportunity (depending on your point of view). But that doesn't mean that women have turned off their attraction triggers when it comes to men in positions of authority. I know of a young woman who was so enamoured of her boss that she entered his office one afternoon, inserted a CD of Johnny Cash songs into his computer, and then performed a strip tease for him, accompanied by the song "Ring of Fire." Apparently, he hadn't sufficiently reacted to her previous – more subtle – hints. Before the performance, the boss had enjoyed flirting with this young lady. Afterward, he was *all* business *all* the time.

Though it's natural to be attracted to married men and bosses, that doesn't mean you should get involved with them. If you continually attract these types of men, but don't *want* to attract them, learn to recognize why. If bosses and married men continually hit on you, you may be transmitting signals that you want sex and/or a romantic relationship with them.

Other "Problem" Types

Some women are drawn to younger men, and there's nothing wrong with that, provided you aren't hoping to settle down and start a family any time soon. For one thing, men *and* women are marrying much later today than they did a couple of generations ago. Therefore, dating anyone under 30 is risky business for marriage-minded women. It's even riskier if you're targeting twenty-something men. Men have no biological clocks, and as I mentioned earlier, they're essentially grown boys. Few men get married unless they feel they have something to gain from the union. Men value their freedom above all – including their annoying habits, senseless hobbies and boyhood friendships. Many men also harbour the mystical belief that the next woman they date will be "better" than the last one.

By the time most men are ready to settle down (somewhere between 25 and posthumous) they have mentally agreed to trade their freedom for the love of a good woman and the emotional security a long-term relationship will bring. This means that you are less likely to find ready-to-marry men who are under 25. Many young men are willing to commit to long-term relationships, but far fewer are willing to put a ring on your finger.

I've encountered dozens of women who've gotten involved with one young man after another, with *none* of the relationships leading to marriage. Some of these women are now in their mid-40s. Some of their relationships lasted three to five years. Most of their boyfriends were perfectly willing to live with the women, but could not be persuaded to get married – no matter what. The only thing these men had in common was that they were all under 30 and none felt ready for marriage and children.

The one common thread connecting all of these *women*, however, is that they tended to be the dominant partners in the relationship – in much the way a mother has more power in the relationship with her son. I'm not saying these women behaved like actual mothers toward these "boys" – only that they were the lead partner: more responsible, more mature, more decisive, and often the bigger money earner. These women didn't nag their would-be mates to dress warmly and clean the gutters, but they *did* hold most of the power in the relationship, and that's rarely a good thing.

Since most men prefer to achieve a 50/50 power balance in relationships (if not more), men who date older women often (unconsciously) slip into mother/son mode. And in most relationships between a normal mothers and sons, the day will come when the boy cuts the umbilical cord to pursue his future wife. On numerous occasions, I've seen younger men live with older women for years, and then suddenly end the relationship. A few months later, the ex-boyfriend meets a younger woman and decides to get married. This usually leaves the abandoned older woman confused, despairing and even more desperate. She's devoted lots of time to building a relationship with the young man – only to get dumped and watch him marry a younger woman in a year or so.

She often thinks, "Something must be wrong with me ... but what?!"

Be of good cheer. There's something wrong with you, but it's easy to fix. Stop dating men under the age of 30! Start dating men closer to your own age. I know this isn't the easiest task if you're divorced or widowed, since there are fewer 40+ bachelors, but it's better than dedicating what's left of your youth and beauty to men who will use you as a "test wife" before spreading their wings to locate the real deal.

Gay men. It's not common for women to mistakenly date gay men, but it happens. In the overwhelming majority of cases, a woman hooks up with a gay man who doesn't yet realize that he's homosexual, or who he thinks he's bisexual and wants to explore "the other side of the fence." (Most bisexuals are primarily attracted to members of one sex – not both equally.) These awkward romances usually occur during the teenage years or because a woman without fully-functional "gadar" hopes that her sexually-undeclared friend will want to form a romantic relationship.

If you are exclusively attracted to gay men, your situation merits psychological counselling. Seriously. You don't really think you're going to "convert" them, do you? Even if you establish a sexual relationship with a gay man, you won't erase his innate attraction to other men. Before the advent of the modern gay rights movement, it was common for homosexual men to get married and perform their husbandly duties with their wives. Playwright Oscar Wilde and composer Peter Tchaikovsky are two well-known examples. But that didn't shut down their sexual orientation.

More recently, there was a nice woman who married a man (a declared bisexual), and they settled down into a suburban routine just outside Chicago. After 12 years of marriage, the man suddenly separated from his wife, and moved to New York to pursue a singing career – not to mention a host of young men. (He'd warned his wife that this might happen someday, but she convinced herself that they were *destined* to be together – that she could keep him straight.)

I don't advise that you get involved with gay men.

Players are a frequent cause of heartbreak among women. This is a guy who is stuck in the adolescent phase of male development, which means that his only goal is sexual gratification and conquest. Players deliberately treat women badly, usually abandoning them after one night of sex. When it comes to relationships, players don't want them. Instead, they are entirely fixated on seducing women – on playing the *attraction & pickup game* for the game's sake alone.

Players represent a minority of men, and should not be confused with men who are merely horny (i.e., all other men) and attempting to fulfil their primitive "prime directive" of having sex with any woman who will allow it.

How do you distinguish between your basic horny man and a player?

Well, players are usually dressed in clothing that distinguishes them from the other men in the room. In addition, they often wear unusual accessories (hats, ties and jewellery) that serve as "conversation starters." This is a technique recommended by *Mystery* – the star of the reality show *The Pick-Up Artist* and author of numerous books on seduction. (Mystery often wears a top hat and goggles.) Players may not be handsome, but they know how to deliver subtle chat-up lines, position themselves as desirable catches, and manipulate every female attraction trigger through a combination of speech and body language.

In a word, players are *smooth* – much more confident and self-assured than the average man. They *always* know what to say, how to say it, and how to quickly escalate relationships from that of total strangers to "bed buddies." Whereas the average man will respond to your cues to take things slowly, since he's interested in a romance that will last longer than one night, the Player will make it obvious that he wants to have sex as soon as possible. The Player both entices (some women) and makes them feel uncomfortable, because he pushes them toward sex so quickly. This is one more reason why you shouldn't drink too much when looking for a guy. Your compromised powers of reasoning will make you easier prey for the Players.

In general, Players only want to seduce the most beautiful women. Of course, every man's definition of beautiful is different, so this doesn't mean that you'll be ignored by players if you don't have supermodel good looks. In fact, Players often appeal to a woman's self-consciousness about her appearance by heaping praise on her. As long as you don't convince yourself that you aren't pretty enough, smart enough or interesting enough to attract the men you want, it will be much harder for Players to manipulate you.

Chapter 5: Why His Sudden Loss of Interest?

Q: *Why does a man have a clear conscience?*
A: *Because it's never used.*

Unlike women, men have a tendency to disappear when they are unhappy in a relationship. Instead of phoning or text messaging a woman with the news that she's been dumped (or saying, "We need to talk"), men are sucked into a black hole from which no sights, sounds or other sensory data ever escape. In other words, they become ghosts. My website readers often ask me to explain these mysterious male disappearances and/or sudden losses of interest.

As a public service, I've created a list of common reasons why men vanish from the face of the Earth and/or why their interest sometimes evaporates overnight.

- ✓ He is still obsessing over a former girlfriend or ex-wife. Be grateful that he has disappeared or lost interest, and will no longer compare you to this ideal of feminine perfection (or pure evil).

- ✓ He's decided that you aren't the one. In which case, *he* wasn't the one.

✓ He was only interested in sex, and has gotten his fill. (See *Player* in Chapter 4.)

✓ He's married or has a girlfriend, and was seeking a "friend with benefits." However, a complication suddenly arose – for example, you just asked him to leave his wife or girlfriend, the other woman is growing suspicious, etc.

✓ You hurt or angered him.

✓ You captured too much power in the relationship.

✓ He is stressed over his career, finances or another priority, and can't cope with a relationship at this time.

✓ You've been diagnosed as a dick tease. This could come under the "hurt or angered" heading, but since dick teasing is such a grievous offense in the male mind, it deserves a bullet point of its own.

Men hate to break up with women. I'm sure many women feel the same about breaking up with men, but it's hard to tell. They seem to relish the opportunity to speak calmly and rationally while reciting the list of injuries the man has inflicted, or while giving a 45-minute speech that could have be summarized with, "It's not you. It's me." I'm almost *certain* that a woman came up with that last bit.

In any case, men are usually non-confrontational when it comes to women, and prefer to evaporate rather than conduct a formal breakup. Also, men expect that the women they dump will get overly emotional, making them feel like jerks. Men hate to feel like jerks. Of course, not every woman will respond to a break-up with tears and anger, but most men expect that they will. Men plan for the worst-case scenario – one that involves embarrassing scenes in restaurants, calls to the police, suicide threats, etc.

A man is *most* likely to disappear without warning if you hurt his feelings or make him angry. Men hate feeling vulnerable or powerless, and strong *emotions* make men feel vulnerable *and* powerless. Despite 50 years of progress in eliminating gender stereotypes, most men are *still* not taught how to cope with their emotions. Quite the opposite: men are taught that it's acceptable to respond to negative situations with a combination of anger and silence. This is the *Vito Corleone Syndrome*. If you've seen *Godfather II*, and remember how Vito treated his wife after she divorced him, you know *exactly* what I mean.

So, men tend to oscillate between shouting and silence. And when they decide to end a relationship, many prefer to skip town to avoid a confrontation. I'm not saying they *will* disappear – only that they prefer to do this. In reality, many men will face the music, and conduct the painful face-to face breakup. They know it's the right (and manly) thing to do. But plenty of others disappear until "the heat is off" – until they think you've gotten over them.

Please note that the odds of a man simply disappearing *decrease* the longer the relationship lasts. He's most likely to disappear, instead of issuing a formal announcement, if you've only been dating for a month or so. As time passes, the odds *increase* that you will stay together or – if he *does* decide to end things – he'll tell you about it. He might even have an explanation, if he's the self-aware type.

By the way, I'm aware that my list of reasons for male vanishing acts applies to women, too. But in my experience, women who wish to end relationships will become unresponsive to phone calls, emails, etc. *before* the "couple" has *mutually* agreed that they have entered a partnership, not afterward. If a woman's going to vanish, she usually does so early in the game – after realizing that she made a mistake in encouraging the man's affections. Most often, this occurs a few weeks (or days) after the first date. Also, women have *many* more reasons for ending relationships than men – at least, reasons they're able to identify and articulate.

If your boyfriend hasn't ended things with you, but is running emotionally "hot and cold," it's possible that he likes you as a person, but isn't sexually attracted to you. Hence, he is probably torn between wanting to spend time together and running away. Men also run hot and cold when the opposite is true – when they enjoy sex with a woman, but little else. If your boyfriend runs hot and cold for an extended period of time, it's probably because he has big doubts about the relationship. If not, there's only one other explanation for his hot-and-cold attitude.

Hyper-Concentration

Men have trouble focusing on more than one priority at a time, especially when the priorities involve career, money, family and so forth. More important, when the typical man is searching for solutions to his problems or is distracted by pressing issues, he can develop an almost superhuman ability to focus on them – to the exclusion of everything else. For example, when I'm responding to an especially difficult question from one of my readers, *nothing* that happens in my immediate environment can shake my concentration – nothing.

On many occasions, my girlfriends have to literally slap the back of my head to break my concentration. Shouting and waving their arms won't work. Then, even after they manage to tear me away from the computer and engage me in (what they think) is a conversation, my brain is still so focused on the other priorities that I will appear disinterested and distracted during the ensuing "conversation."

I refer to this phenomenon as "hyper-concentration."

Feel free to blame my Cro-Magnon ancestors for this "problem," as successful hunting requires patience and a near-obsessive focus on the quarry. Aside from hunting, I believe this trait still comes in handy, though I understand why women find it annoying and worrisome. When your boyfriend or husband is distracted and uncommunicative for weeks or months, you can't help wondering if there's something amiss in the relationship.

If your husband or boyfriend seems quiet and distracted for an extended period, all you can do is ask him what's on his mind and try to help solve his problem(s) to the best of your ability. If that doesn't work, give him time to work things out on his own. Trying to get his mind off the situation doesn't help very often, and may even annoy him, especially when he expresses a desire for "space" and "time."

Note: please don't confuse hyper-concentration with "flooding," a phenomenon characterized by a complete mental shutdown. I'll cover this topic in the next chapter.

For a man, sex *does* establish a bond with a woman, but the bond isn't strong enough to keep him coming back if he doesn't *really* fancy you as a person. If he isn't interested in the complete package that is *you*, showing up at your door wearing sexy lingerie may put some "yowsers" back in his trousers, but it won't save a failing relationship. It's time to move on.

Chapter 6: Men Are from Vulcan

Men are like Mascara.
They usually run at the first sign of emotion.

Male Communication Styles

First, it's important to understand that men are not from Mars.

Since most men are taught to control their emotions, it's more accurate to say, "Men are from Vulcan" – the home planet of *Star Trek's* Mr. Spock. For the record, Vulcans (male and female) *do* possess emotions – powerful and sometimes violent impulses that nearly destroyed their race in the distant past. To preserve their civilization, Vulcans learned to control (some might say *suppress*) their emotions, and rely entirely on logic and reason. Every seven years, however, male Vulcans essentially go into heat. During the "Pon Farr," every male loses his capacity for logic, and unleashes every primitive and passionate impulse in an effort to win a mate – or die trying. (He will literally die if he doesn't find a mate.) On occasion, the latter outcome is helped along when two Vulcan men fight to the death for the hand of a maiden.

Sound familiar?

Of course.

Star Trek creator Gene Roddenberry tended to incorporate selected human traits into each of his alien races. In the case of the Vulcans, he assigned everything that's calm, rational and "left brained" about human beings, except when it comes time for dating and mating. Then, male Vulcans go berserk – just like human beings (both male *and* female) often go berserk whenever romance is in the air.

In terms of their communication style, men are not nearly as good as women at articulating their thoughts and feelings. Men are problem solvers. Ask a man to solve your problems, and he'll quickly present a range of options, supported by spreadsheets, maps and a PowerPoint presentation. Talk to a man about how rotten your day was, in the hopes of eliciting sympathy and active listening, and you're out of luck.

Most men don't know how to offer sympathy and emotional support. Unless you ask him to propose solutions to the *problems* that caused your rotten day, or would like him to put everything into perspective, he'll just stand there, shrugging his shoulders.

A word on what *perspective* means to men. In the larger scheme of things, anything short of death, life-threatening health conditions or financial ruin is not considered a "disaster" to the typical man. In the male universe, any challenge that doesn't pose the risk of imminent death and material deprivation will not garner overt sympathy or an emergency plan of action. Consider this real-life example:

WOMAN: [Slams the front door and chucks her purse on the sofa, where the boyfriend is lying, watching TV.] What a lousy day!

MAN: Hmm. What's wrong?

WOMAN: My idiot boss had me in his office for two hours, rambling on and on about meeting deadlines and getting organized. He didn't say anything he hasn't said a hundred times before, but now I'm behind schedule because he wasted half the day blabbing!

MAN: That sucks. [Returns his gaze to the TV]

WOMAN: I am so stressed out. I don't know what to do!

MAN: You want a beer?

WOMAN: I want my boss to die!

MAN: Why don't you apply for his job? He's retiring soon, right? Once you're the boss, nobody can waste your time.

WOMAN: I don't *want* his job.

MAN: Oh.

WOMAN: I want you to help me instead of sitting on your lazy ass, watching TV.

MAN: I *was* helping.

WOMAN: Shut up! [Storms off]

In this example, the woman merely wanted a sympathetic ear and a comforting arm around her shoulder to help her "vent" and unwind. Instead, the man offered alcoholic beverages and career advice – both practical solutions, but hardly what she wanted from him. He literally cannot understand why she's angry, since *he* would feel better if someone offered him a similar solution to this problem. Meanwhile, she probably thinks that he doesn't give a fig about her feelings, because he didn't seem to empathize with her situation. This sort of miscommunication is typical.

At other times, men and women come into conflict when the woman expects her man to *know* her well enough to anticipate her every desire or pinpoint the reason that she's upset at any given moment. Every man I've known has complained that he sometimes receives a tongue-lashing when he doesn't take his girlfriend to her favourite restaurant without her having to ask. You see, he was supposed to *know* – either by reading her facial expressions, body language or tea leaves – that she *wanted* to have dinner at the Market Street Inn that evening. The fact that he didn't perceive her desire within several seconds *proves* he doesn't care about her feelings.

Even worse, from the male point of view, is when a woman plunks into a chair, folds her arms, and prepares to burst into tears. When the man invariably asks what's wrong, he's already made a fatal mistake. He should already know what's wrong, whether he caused the upset or not. This also applies to birthday, Christmas and anniversary gifts – in fact, gifts for every occasion. If the man does not buy the perfect gift, this reveals that he doesn't understand who she is at a fundamental level.

There is a single, blanket explanation for why men rarely anticipate a woman's desires, recognize when and why she is upset and/or choose poor birthday, anniversary and holiday gifts: *Men don't do "subtle."* They won't recognize subtle hints about your desires, they will often ignore your emotional states because they don't know how to handle emotions, and they will rarely catch hints about gifts you'd like them to purchase in the future. You may as well ask a man to read your mind as anticipate your wishes, memorize gift lists and identify your moods (much less the reasons for them).

This doesn't make men bad people. It simply makes them … men.

I have no doubt that a man invented the saying, "actions speak louder than words," because men truly believe this. They prefer to *demonstrate* love and commitment rather than profess it – very often. Men don't like to use the word *love* because: (A) it is an emotion, and (B) they think that words mean nothing unless they are supported by actions. This is how they were raised from boyhood.

If you want your man to become a better listener and to support your feelings, you'll need to train him. But first you must get him to agree that emotions matter. This may not be that hard. Just tell him that he must respect and respond to your feelings because your feelings are important to *you*. Therefore, if he values you, he will also value and acknowledge your feelings – even if he doesn't know how to deal with them. You can always tell him how to deal with your feelings while he's in training. For example, if you want a hug, ask for one. If you want a shoulder to cry on, ask for it. Later, you can take off the training wheels, and he should be able to respond automatically to your emotional needs.

Men respond well to simple requests, but not subtle hints. For this reason, you should *NEVER* read too much into what a man says. If you've been dating someone for a few weeks, and he concludes a text message with "C U L8er," do not assume for a *millisecond* that this is code for "I am breaking up with you." It means exactly what it says – "I will see you later. This is the conclusion of the text." For the most part, men are simple, honest creatures without wile or guile. (*Players* and *Nice Guys* are the exceptions to this rule.)

How to Argue (Not Quarrel) with a Man

According to research psychologist John Gottman, most couple's therapy fails because conventional techniques don't work. The biggest myth is that learning to *resolve* conflict puts couples on the road to a happy relationship.

One technique that he singles out is *active listening.* This is where a therapist asks one partner to make a statement on how she feels when her boyfriend does this or that. She uses "I" statements to tell the boyfriend how his behaviour affects her feelings. While she talks, the boyfriend listens carefully, so he can later summarize what she said. This proves that he's been *actively* listening to her criticism.

For example, you might say to your boyfriend, "I feel you don't want to commit to spending time together. You never agree to weekend plans in advance. You always wait until Friday." After you're done talking, your boyfriend is supposed to summarize what you just said to *validate* your feelings. Allegedly, this opens up the lines of communication in a safe and secure environment.

The problem with this approach, says Gottman, is that your boyfriend is *not* a therapist coolly listening to third-party criticism. *He's* the one being criticized by your "I feel" statements. Some people can take this kind of ego-busting barrage, but many people get upset. And this only aggravates the underlying tensions. That's why *active listening* fails so often.

This doesn't mean that you and your boyfriend should avoid arguments. *Avoiding* arguments is the *worst* thing you can do. Many healthy relationships erupt in shouting matches every so often. It's *how* you argue that makes the difference. *Managing* conflict – arguing by certain rules – is what distinguishes a healthy relationship from one that's on life support. Conflict *resolution* isn't what saves relationships. Conflict *management* does. (Some couples spend their whole lives managing conflicts, because some arguments can never be resolved.)

Gottman has developed seven principles to help people avoid what he calls the "four horsemen" of failed relationships. When these four horsemen come into play on a regular basis, you're relationship is in serious trouble.

The first horseman is *criticism*. I'm not talking about *complaints* directed at your partner, but overall criticism – using global statements such as, "Simon, you are such a gullible idiot." That's a criticism. As opposed to, "Simon, I don't think this email is really from a Nigerian prince who needs your help accessing his fortune."

The second horseman is *contempt*. This is especially destructive, because even if one partner is *not* getting emotional about criticism, now he's getting bombarded with sarcasm. Sarcastic remarks show that one person holds the other in contempt. She insists on winning arguments by ripping her boyfriend a new one.

Contempt often leads to the third horseman: *defensiveness*. In most cases, being defensive only escalates conflict. That's because defensiveness switches blame back to the other person. "I only fall for scam emails from Nigerian princes because you spend so much money that *someone* needs to keep us out of the poor house!"

That's defensiveness.

Now, if my girlfriend were to keep pounding away at my ego, telling me how stupid I was to respond to these scam emails, I might eventually tune out. This is known as *stonewalling*, and it's the fourth horseman. More than women, men are prone to emotional overload. They literally shut down. There's a biological reason behind this phenomenon, but I'll skip that. Suffice it to say that when men stonewall, it's like a computer screen that freezes. (This is also called *emotional flooding*.)

All four horseman may have arrived at the door, but that doesn't mean the relationship is doomed – not if you use Gottman's seven principles.

None of the principles is especially mind-blowing. Take the first principle – enhancing your "love maps." All this means is that partners should get to know something about each other – their likes and dislikes, fears and hopes, etc. It's about getting to know someone as well as you can. If you can't name your partner's friends and co-workers, and don't know his favourite foods, despite the fact that he talks about them every day, you're either the world's worst listener or you don't place much value on knowing your partner.

The second principle is *nurturing your fondness and admiration*. This involves tapping into your history as a couple to draw out the wonderful moments. You recall the reasons you became a couple or got married in the first place.

After a while, almost everyone starts to take his/her partner for granted. Too often, people focus on what annoys them about the other person instead of reminding themselves of what they love. So Gottman recommends that you regularly refresh your positive memories. This is what nurturing fondness and admiration is about – especially if you've hit a snag in the relationship.

If you constantly obsess over your boyfriend's negative qualities, you could end up hating him. If your boyfriend snores, and you spend too much time thinking about the *damned snoring*, you might hit him with a sledgehammer one night. You'd forget that you really love him, despite his flaws.

Even if the horsemen have already upset your relationship, there's still time to repair things – *if* you employ the third principle, which is turning *toward* each other, not away from each other. It means staying *connected* during all the humdrum days that comprise your life together. It's about asking how his day was when he returns from the office, and actually listening to what he says. It means showing that you value your boyfriend – even in small ways. You thank him for a delicious meal, or for doing the dishes, and stuff like that. Express your appreciation to your partner in little ways.

If you're not turning toward each other, you're not allowing your partner to *influence* you, which is Gottman's fourth principle. One common reason that couples experience tension is a lack of power sharing and mutual influencing. In my experience, it's rare to see relationships in which power is shared equally. It's *more common* to see a dominant and a submissive partner – or two people locked in a power struggle. Many people say their relationships are equal partnerships, but that's bunk. People only say that because it's politically correct. Somebody usually wears the pants.

So, couples need to share power. If you ask your boyfriend to clean the bathroom, he does. If he doesn't have time at that moment, he does it later. He doesn't whine about it being women's work. And you don't scream that it has to be done *now*. If it has to be done now, and he doesn't have time, you should do it yourself. Cut each other slack when it comes to sharing power and responsibility in the relationship.

Also, search for common ground to help manage conflicts. You don't have to give away your personal power. You don't have to *cave in* whenever your boyfriend makes demands or gets upset. You don't have to cop out with "Yes honey," "Whatever you say, honey." Just keep your mind open to influence and input.

If your boyfriend (or you) refuses to be influenced or compromise, you have a problem. That's exactly what Gottman found among couples where mutual influencing (and power sharing) wasn't occurring. When Gottman had newlywed couples discuss areas of conflict or talk about their histories together, he was struck by a big difference between the sexes. Where wives would sometimes express anger or negative emotions toward the husbands, they usually tried to calm things down or match their husbands' level of anger during arguments. It was rare for them to actually escalate the quarrelling.

But 65% of husbands said or did things that escalated their wives negativity – usually by engaging in contempt, criticism, stonewalling or defensiveness. In other words, instead of listening to the wife's complaints and trying to defuse negativity, the typical husband refused to accept her influence and tried to crush her point of view.

At the end of the day, people who refuse to accept influence are asking for trouble. Whether the couple gets into vicious arguments or drives negativity underground by avoiding arguments, the romance is doomed. Accepting influence is the only way to *solve* the solvable arguments.

It's also important for couples to abide by the ground rules when they discuss sensitive subjects, so Gottman suggests five ways to prevent discussions from escalating into nuclear wars.

Step one is to use a "soft start-up" to launch the discussion. Introduce a problem you're having with a partner in a gentle, non-confrontational way. For example, last summer, I was at a female friend's house while she was having her irrigation system repaired. One of the workmen was digging holes in her lawn, looking for breaks in the underground pipes. At one point, he began shovelling dirt onto her flower bed without thinking. She said, "Excuse me, would you please avoid shovelling dirt on my flowers?" The workman hadn't noticed what he was doing, so he apologized and removed the dirt from her flowers. *That's* a soft start-up to addressing an area of conflict.

Meanwhile, my friend's husband was supervising the repairs, and at one point, he tripped over her herb garden and landed on the oregano. Instead of saying, "Please be careful around my herbs" or "Don't hurt yourself," she tore into him. "What the hell's the matter with you! Don't you have any sense? You've ruined my oregano!" She didn't show her own *husband* the same courtesy she'd just extended to a stranger!

Obviously, it's better to launch discussions with the soft start-up. But where do you go from there? That's where step two comes in. You learn to make and receive "repair attempts." This means you make and receive attempts to soothe feelings and validate different points of view. So if doing housework is a sore spot in my relationship, my girlfriend might go on the defensive immediately. "I do plenty of things around this house!" To make a repair attempt, I'll respond by saying, "Yes, you do." I might even offer examples of things she does around the house. If she accepts the repair attempt, she will calm down and listen further.

Step three is to soothe yourself and each other. This is especially important for men. As I mentioned earlier, men are more prone to emotional flooding than women. It takes longer for them to calm down – emotionally and physically – once they become stressed. Their hearts are racing, they're sweating and they may be holding their breaths. This reaction is probably a holdover from those damned Cro-Magnon times when it was important that men remain vigilant to threats for longer periods.

If one person gets flooded and stonewalls, the other person should stop the discussion, and suggest that everyone take a time out until the dust settles. Taking a break is a basic rule of arguing. You can't compromise if emotions are running high.

Compromise is step four. Once an argument gets too heated, it becomes hard to accept influence, because you're now locked in a battle of criticism and defensiveness. You've set aside logic in favour of an emotional slugging match. What started as a problem-solving attempt turns into a war to win the argument.

Step five is recognizing that some problems will never be resolved. In these cases, you have to learn to cope with the "gridlock." The best way to do that is to keep the lines of communication open and demonstrate respect for the other person's feelings.

For example, I know a couple where the wife cannot stand the smell of seafood. The wife gets physically ill at the smell of seafood. But her husband absolutely *loves* seafood – crabs, lobster, clams, mussels, and every kind of fish. For years, he refused to stop cooking seafood, despite the fact his wife begged him. She'd burst into tears whenever he brought home a bag of clams, even after he lit scented candles and opened the windows. The quarrels went on for years until, eventually, the husband agreed to only eat seafood in restaurants. That doesn't bother her as much. And the wife agreed not to complain about the "stench" when he ordered seafood in restaurants.

So neither is *completely* happy, but neither is completely miserable.

That's one of the definitions of compromise.

Chapter 7: The Keys to a Lasting Relationship

Q: *What's the difference between a man and a messy room.*

A: *You can straighten up a messy room.*

This chapter is a little unusual. Here, I don't focus on the male mind, but on the *Five Critical Factors* needed to build and maintain a healthy, long-term relationship.

> ➤ Mutual physical attraction.
> ➤ Common values.
> ➤ Common goals.
> ➤ Similar or complementary personalities.
> ➤ Common interests. (Believe it or not, this is the *least* important factor.)

Mutual physical attraction is a given. As much as we *want* to believe that personality, values and goals are the deciding factors in choosing a mate, they aren't. When a man and a woman aren't *that* sexually attracted to each other, the best they can hope for is an enduring friendship – even if the friendship leads to a marriage. Believe me, there are *lots* of people who settle for someone they don't find *that* attractive – more people than you probably imagine.

And when they're honest about it, they will admit that the sexual component is sorely missing from their relationships.

People who have "settled" with regard to appearance may be genuinely happy in every other respect, but no romance can ever flourish in the absence of strong physical attraction. I'm not saying that your future husband must be *the* most drop-dead gorgeous man you've ever seen and the most fantastic lover known to humankind. Let's be realistic here. At the same time, you should *want* to have sex with him at least twice a month – without forcing him to beg, crawl and/or wear a paper bag over his head.

Common values are critical to any relationship – not just romantic ones – since your values express your individual worldview and priorities. They define who you are in relation to the rest of humanity, and what's important to you. If you're a devout Christian who believes it's important to "treat others as you would have them treat you," you will *not* be compatible with a man who sincerely believes that "It's a dog-eat-dog world. You have to stick it to the other guy before he sticks it to you." If you try to maintain a relationship with such a man, you will have to cope with more irresolvable conflicts than Israel and the Arab world. It's likely that you'll spend most of your time arguing and quarrelling, because you are two fundamentally different human beings.

Determining someone's values takes time, so don't rush to judgment. For one thing, there are millions of professed Christians, Muslims, Hindus and Buddhists who pay lip service to their religions, but may as well worship Al Capone. Conversely, I've known some atheists who were quite moral and even spiritually enlightened.

On the other hand, if your boyfriend insists from Day One that he never wants children, while you dream of raising a family, you are *never* going to reach agreement without a values compromise. (And most people don't compromise on values.) Differences in values are usually too important to be assigned to the list of perpetual conflicts that you'll just have to cope with for the rest of your lives. Most of the time, they are deal breakers.

People's values *can* change, but don't *expect* this to happen, or try to make it happen. For example, young men tend to value friendships over family and children. (Another reason I advise against dating younger men.) As they grow older, however, most men come to value family and children over their friendships. Aside from this example, I can't think of another "values shift" that you can ever count on.

Common goals often go hand in hand with common values – e.g., the desire to raise a family, to focus on your careers, or to *experience* new people, places and ideas instead of *acquiring* material objects. In general, goals represent the ways that you express your values in the material world. Hence, the career-minded man will spend a lot of time in the office, will focus on developing strategies and tactics to win promotions, and he probably *won't* spend time taking classes in meditation, yoga or reading books on existential philosophy. I suppose the one key difference between values and goals is this: Even if a man has values that conflict with yours, you may share common goals if he never *acts* on the values that you don't like. For instance, the man who believes that it's a "dog eat dog world" could make a good partner if another one of his values prevents him from actually "sticking it" to other people.

Compatible Personality Types and Traits

Similar or complementary personality types. There are literally dozens – if not hundreds – of books on this subject, and nearly as many systems, labels and categories of personality that are supposedly great matches – or at least compatible. I recommend two books on this topic. One is entitled, *Why Him? Why Her?* by Rutgers University research professor Helen Fisher.

Based on her extensive research into brain chemistry, Fisher divides people into four basic personality types. These types are pegged to each person's relative levels of certain bio-chemicals – oestrogen, testosterone, serotonin and dopamine. She also explains why certain personality types are more compatible than others.

The four types are:

1. Directors
2. Negotiators
3. Explorers
4. Builders

Everyone has these chemicals inside him. To some degree, therefore, everyone displays these four sets of personality traits. But since we are all "mixed" with different amounts of these chemicals, some personality traits are more dominant. Fisher categorizes people by their dominant and second-most dominant traits. Everyone is assigned an A/B classification. For example: you might be a Director/Explorer while your boyfriend is a Negotiator/Explorer, a Builder/Negotiator and so forth.

Since every person is an individual cocktail of these four ingredients, you can't stereotype people based on the A/B category. But you *can* gain insight into their *prominent* personality traits by knowing their A/B category. This gives you a head start in the dating and mating game. In some cases, you can even identify someone's personality type by his physical appearance.

For example, Negotiators have higher oestrogen levels than other types. People with smooth skin, smaller noses and soft round faces (baby faces) tend to have higher oestrogen levels. Directors, with higher levels of testosterone, have facial features that often include prominent cheekbones and square faces – like Kirk Douglas or Patrick Stewart (Fisher hasn't yet identified any physical characteristics associated with the other personality types.)

Explorers, with their higher dopamine levels, exhibit restlessness and energy. They are intellectual and physical thrill seekers, and like to travel and experience new things. They also tend to be impulsive, optimistic, creative, generous, flexible and very curious about the world around them. On the negative side, Explorers can be so irreverent that they insult people's beliefs without thinking. They can also come off as cynical and flip. And because they're impulsive, they tend to be late for appointments, including dates.

Directors are logical and analytical, and very direct in their speech. A Director will tell you what he thinks – to the point of being rude. Directors are focused, take-charge people who enjoy leading. This is the guy you want leading your army, because he's tough-minded and decisive, and his decisions are based on his powers of reasoning. The biggest problem with the Director is that he can be so reserved that he never expresses any feelings. For that reason, Directors tend to have only a few close friends. The Director can seem closed off and impenetrable. He might come across as calm and emotionally reserved 95% of the time, and then BLAM! All the feelings that he's kept pent up inside will suddenly explode in a violent outburst.

Negotiators are the philosopher kings. The main characteristic of the Negotiator is imagination and intuition. They tend to be people persons, and big-picture thinkers. They're also empathetic, sociable, pleasant and good at conversation. On the negative side, they can be too trusting, opening up to the wrong people at the wrong time.

Finally, we have the Builder. Fisher refers to these people as pillars of society. These people tend to have higher levels of serotonin. They exhibit remarkable persistence, reliability and a play-by-the-rules mentality. They are usually devoted to institutions and organizations that comprise the building blocks of their societies – family, church, volunteer organizations, companies and so on. They have a great deal of respect for authority and for experts, for law and order, routines and schedules, and for precise, logical and detailed thinking.

Some people believe that opposites attract, while others think that similarity attracts. In my view, both views have some merit. And Fisher agrees. She says, for example, that Directors and Negotiators come together quite often, and they make fantastic couples – even though Directors are Type-A personalities and Negotiators are laid back and intuitive. In many cases, these traits complement each other.

On the other hand, if you get two Builders together, they'll probably get along, too. They might sit down every Friday night at their favourite restaurant and map out chores and leisure-time activities. Since Builder's love routines and predictability, they might not need to even map anything out. They'll do the same things every weekend.

Unlike the Fisher's book, *The Love Compatibility Book* by Edward Hoffman and Marcella Bakur Weiner, focuses on "The Big 12 Traits Affecting Intimacy." These personality traits have less to do with brain chemistry, and more to do with values and temperament. At least, that's how I see it. According to the authors, the right combination of these traits can make the relationship, and the wrong combination can break it. The Big 12 Traits Affecting Intimacy are:

1. Need for Companionship
2. Idealism

3. Emotional Intensity
4. Spontaneity
5. Libido
6. Nurturance
7. Materialism
8. Extroversion
9. Aestheticism
10. Activity Level
11. Subjective Well-Being
12. Intellectualism

The need for companionship is a core trait, because some people need to have intimate conversations with their partners all the time, or they want the partner around most of the time. Other people are more independent or emotionally distant. They would feel smothered by someone who's always keen to share deep secrets and private thoughts. Obviously, most people are somewhere in between these two extremes.

Idealism comes down to whether you view human beings as inherently good and trustworthy, or think that people are motivated by fear, greed, envy and their egos.

Emotional intensity means that some people are more emotional than others, and big differences can cause problems. If your boyfriend is always crying whenever he watched romantic comedies, and you think this makes him a sissy, then he's probably too emotionally intense for you.

Spontaneity is the opposite of routine and predictability, and having a boyfriend who wants to do things on a spur of the moment can be irritating if you're not spontaneous yourself – or at least tolerant of it.

Libido is all about the person's sex drive. If you're dating someone who isn't as interested in sex as you, you have a built-in problem with this relationship. Of course, people's sex drives often change over time. You might start dating a man who wants to spend every night doing the positions in the Kama Sutra. Then, after a couple of years, he decides that once a month is more than enough.

Nurturance has to do with whether you like to be pampered and taken care of. One woman might like to pamper her boyfriend while another expects him to pamper *her.*

Extroversion describes people who feel energized in group settings and by interacting with people. They look outside of themselves for inspiration and to form their views of the world. Introverts look inward and might feel awkward being around groups of people for very long – or at all. That doesn't mean that extroverts and introverts can't get along. After all, it's just one personality trait and there are different degrees of introversion and extroversion.

Materialism is a pretty self-explanatory trait, so I'll just say that people who lean toward materialism may not be good matches with those who are more spiritually inclined. On the other hand, you never know. Two people may have so many other personality traits and values in common that it won't make much difference.

Aestheticism is about the degree to which someone appreciates art, music and anything else that can be sensed and enjoyed for its inherent beauty. Everyone occasionally takes a moment to appreciate the colours of an amazing sunset, or is moved by a piece of music. But some people live for those moments, while others don't pay much attention. It's often a good idea to search for someone with a similar appreciation for literature and the arts.

Activity level is also pretty self-explanatory. Some people appreciate relaxing moments and taking life slow. Other people can't seem to find their "off switch." A woman with a high activity level may be easily bored by a low-activity man; while the man will get exhausted just watching the high-activity woman run around like a mechanical wind-up toy.

Subjective well-being can encompass a lot of things, but it really hinges on whether you're an optimist or a pessimist. Are you the kind of person who believes that everything will eventually work out, or do you expect the other shoe to drop at any moment? If you're an optimist who thinks the universe has a purpose, then you won't want to date someone who's a downer.

The final trait is intellectualism. Do you love to read books and magazines, follow the news, and have discussions about matters of import –politics, economics, science, societal trends? Or do intellectual pursuits make you fall asleep?

Common Interests

Most people operate on the assumption that *Common Interests* are the key to a successful relationship. This simply isn't true. If common interests were the key to compatibility, the human race would have died out around the time men invented sports and weekend hobbies. I know, I know. Some of you ladies enjoy sports and carpentry projects as much (or more) than the men in your lives. The point is, you don't need a boatload of common interests to build a long-term relationship. Of course, it would be nearly impossible to build a relationship if you had *NO* common interests, but what are the odds of that?

My friend Pete is now married to a woman (Linda) who shares only a handful of his interests, and vice versa. Aside from holidays to tropical locales – especially Bermuda and the Caribbean – and a shared interest in swimming and nature hikes, they go their own ways on the weekends. Pete plays golf and tends his vegetable garden during the warmer months in Maryland. Linda loves cross stitching, flower gardening and soap operas. Pete reads history books for pleasure. Linda reads murder mysteries. Pete likes to follow politics in the newspapers, magazines and online. Linda cares so little about politics that Pete practically has to drag her to the voting booth every election season. And so on and so forth.

What they *do* have in common is attraction, values, goals, etc., as well as a half-dozen common interests. Of course, if Pete were still an absolute maniac about sports, which he was in his younger days, Linda has advised that she might never have gotten together with him. This points to a caveat: If one person has a near-obsessive interest in something, and the other person does not – or genuinely *hates* that particular interest – then you have a problem. Of course, *hating* a particular interest isn't really about a lack of common interests. It's a pet peeve that belongs under the heading (maybe) of "incompatible personality types."

Many people are so blinded by their initial attraction that they mistake *lust* for *love*. They don't consider things like values, goals, personality and temperament until there's a huge clash. Seriously. How many of you go on dates thinking, "I'm going to interview this guy over the course of three months to see if his values, goals and personality are compatible – based on a scientific laundry list?" Getting to know somebody in depth takes time. That's what dating is for. It's time that people are supposed to spend learning whether they'll make a good, long-term match.

The biggest problems occur when people are so blinded by looks and a few common interests that they rush into a commitment.

Chapter 8: Hot and Cold Running Ex's

Q: *Why do men chase women they have no intention of marrying?*

A: *For the same reason dogs chase cars they have no intention of driving.*

Many ex-boyfriends will want to maintain a relationship, including a sexual relationship, once a little time has passed after the split. Typical reasons include:

✓ Most men find it harder to start new relationships than continue old ones.

✓ Some men aren't ready to immediately start dating again, and feel more comfortable spending time with the "devil they know."

✓ Most men (and human beings, for that matter) allow their memories of past relationships to become clouded with nostalgia, forgetting the bad times and focusing entirely on the best of times.

✓ If you had a sexual relationship (and the sex was good), he will persuade himself that he wants just one more encore performance to get you out of his system. *Note*: "One more time" often turns into *dozens* more times unless you say "no."

✓ He may be hoping for reconciliation, regardless of who dumped whom.

Let's face it. If you and your boyfriend spent a significant amount of time together, odds are high that you *both* invested plenty of emotional energy in the relationship. That sort of energy doesn't just evaporate the moment one person says, "I think we should see other people" or "It's not you, it's me." If you had an amicable parting of the ways, but (A) decided to remain friends, (B) still have mutual friends, or (C) regularly "bump into" each other, there will be a temptation to relive "the good times" at least once or twice following the break-up – sometimes more.

Unless you or your ex was cheating (or had an eye on someone else), and immediately launches a romance with another person, both of you may be lonely and bored for several weeks or months after the separation. Nostalgia will probably kick in. You will miss the fun, the sex, the companionship, and the desire to feel needed by another human being. What's more, every man wants to *know* that you miss his company. He may be confused, even if *he* dumped *you*. Though he doesn't see a future in the relationship, there had to be *something* about it that he enjoyed. At the very least, he probably still finds you attractive and still cares about you. Therefore, if he hasn't found someone to replace you when you next encounter him, your reunion may be fraught with danger. He may express wistful regrets, and sigh about "what might have been," as his none-too-subtle attempts to get you into bed "one more time."

If this hasn't happened to you already, then you haven't dated enough men. Getting back with your ex – if only for a night – isn't an everyday occurrence, but it happens often enough to deserve a chapter in this book.

I've seen dozens of instances of this phenomenon. In some cases, I've seen ex-couples spend more time together – and probably have more sex – *after* the alleged separation than they did while dating. Some ex-couples go on like this for *years*, which wouldn't be so bad if they were actually considering a reconciliation, or if their pseudo-relationships didn't impede their individual searches for Mr. and Ms. Right.

Sometimes, these ex-couples form co-dependent bonds. Each ex-partner emotionally enables the other to stay in the relationship, even though both people know that the romance isn't going anywhere. Some ex's even offer each other tacit "veto power" over the other's new choice of partner! Believe me, I've seen this happen. It's not a healthy thing to do.

If you have no interest in getting together with your ex, then you have to be strong. You have to break the emotional bonds – or at least the sexual bonds – even if you are still attached to him. Be strong for your sake and his. If you get back with him, you'll only prolong the agony of the break-up, and the eventual (final) separation will probably be *more* painful.

By the time the "ultimate split" occurs, you may be such an emotional wreck that it will kill any chance for a friendship that you might have had. In the meantime, whenever he *does* find someone else, he will disappear with her, and only return if things don't work out. This could become a cycle that's repeated for months or even years: your ex starts dating, it doesn't work out, you get together during his "downtime," and then endure a second, third, fourth, etc. break-up every time he finds a new girlfriend.

Here's a real-life example that combines just about every nightmare scenario you could stuff into a relationship:

One of my acquaintances dated a woman who was 10 years younger than him – a beautiful would-be actress who'd just moved to London to pursue a career in the theatre. (Let's call the man "Gerard" and the woman "Sarah.")

Gerard and Sarah dated for six weeks before she ditched him for another man. He was heartbroken, but moved on after a time. A year later, he changed jobs, and his new office was just a block from a new restaurant where she worked as a waitress. Before long, he was hanging out at the bar after hours, talking old times with her. One night, after Gerard and Sarah consumed enormous amounts of alcohol while talking about what it might be like to "hook up" again; they went back to his place and had sex. This launched "Round 2" of their relationship, which lasted about two months before she called things off. She said she didn't see a future with him, but at the same time, she desperately wanted to remain friends.

Just a few weeks later, however, Sarah nearly found herself homeless. Her flatmate kicked her out following a heated argument. She begged Gerard to let her stay with him until she found a new place, and he foolishly agreed. What happened next was pretty predictable.

Living with Gerard in his one-bedroom flat, the day arrived when a little alcohol and nostalgia once again fuelled some "quality time" between the sheets. Although they both agreed not to get involved again – that this was just a temporary "friends with benefits" arrangement – let's get real. Does anyone seriously believe that two ex's can resume a sexual relationship and then treat each other as mere friends?

I don't think they really believed it, but they quickly formed a co-dependent relationship. Sarah needed a place to stay, and Gerard was lonely and desperate for affection. What's more, it wasn't *his* idea to break up with Sarah either time.

In the months that followed, Sarah dated a succession of men (that was the agreement, after all), which prompted a series of jealous quarrels between the two roommates. Gerard never admitted to being jealous, but who are we kidding, here? By the end of a year, Gerard began dating again, but now it was Sarah's turn to incite the jealous arguments and also argue that his new girlfriend wasn't right for him. It wasn't until 18 months of cohabitation had passed that Sarah finally found the man that she eventually married, and the ultimate split occurred. Instead of enduring yet another jealous argument with Gerard, she simply moved out – into the house of her fiancé. Gerard went back to the girlfriend that Sarah had suggested he dump, and eventually married her.

Gerard and Sarah have not spoken to each other since.

While this may seem like an extreme case, the only unusual feature of the relationship between these ex's is that they lived together for nearly two years. Otherwise, their behaviour is pretty typical of what can happen when a couple doesn't sever the romantic bonds – quickly and with extreme prejudice.

Yes, there are circumstances where things can work out again. But if your ex is saying, "Can I come round and stay the night, and we'll patch things up over breakfast, then just forget it. That's a sign that he just wants some company and an easy lay for a few weeks or months, until he finds someone else. Of course, if he declares that he wants to get engaged or married, or starts romancing you and making a big effort, you may want to give him a second chance. The crucial difference is the man's *intent*. If he's simply giving you some sweet talk in the hopes of assuaging his loneliness, boredom and sexual desires until he finds someone else, it should be pretty obvious. He probably won't talk about engagement or marriage and, if he does, he won't back up the talk with any action.

Never agree to be friends unless both of you agreed to call it quits, and each of you sincerely believes it was best to end the relationship. Keep in mind, however, that even when you agree to be friends, you *will* be hurt and jealous once he finds a new "significant other" – unless you find one first. That's just the way it is. If you can deal with that, then give the friendship a go. But don't say I didn't warn you.

Most guys won't finish a relationship by telling you that they don't love you anymore and never did. Why? Because they care about your feelings, and want you to go out there and find someone else. Men hate to feel guilty, and they don't want to be held responsible for destroying your life. They want to part on good terms. They don't want to say, "I never found you sexy. You didn't excite me. You didn't give me long-term vibes. I found you unattractive. There was just something about you that I knew was wrong for me," etc. These may be his *real* reasons for the break-up, but he won't want to admit that. He will disguise the real reasons.

If a woman said those things to him, he would be devastated. Therefore, most men will never say such things to a woman. They will invent ridiculous and illogical stories to justify the break-up, even if you ask them for the real reasons. If you catch them in a lie, they will invent another story.

Even if you're a supermodel, this doesn't mean all guys are going to find you attractive. Rest assured, there are men who will find you attractive, whatever you look like, but only a minority of men will be well-suited for a long-term relationship.

One more reason for withholding the truth is that men are desperately afraid of *Fatal Attraction* types. Most men are egotistical enough to think that you will become a raving psycho if he gives you his real reasons for dumping you. He will think that you will immediately turn to stalking him, phoning him, making him feel guilty and telling malicious stories about him. Hence, he will want to maintain peace with you. If he told you that he doesn't really find you attractive, this (he thinks) is more likely to make you bitter and attempt to seek revenge. In his mind, this will make you feel used – as if he never had any intention of entering a long-term relationship with you.

Important Tip: *Never* behave like a psycho.

Don't even hint that you may do something psychotic – even if he had an affair with your best friend or your mother. Any "bunny boiling" incidents that you threaten or actually carry out will haunt you for the rest of your life. He will tell his friends, and might even call the police if your threats or actions are particularly heinous.

If you behave like a psychopath, it's possible your friends will learn about this, and maybe even the entire neighbourhood. Restraining orders aren't good for your reputation. In fact, developing a reputation for psychotic behaviour means that you definitely, under no circumstances, stand a chance of reuniting with him or dating any of his friends, or their friends, or friends of their friends, etc. You may have to move a considerable distance, change your usernames on every social networking site, change your phone numbers and maybe even change your name to erase the damage.

Quite simply, men don't like dating psychos or splitting up with them. If they hear rumours that you're a potential psycho a few seconds before asking you out, they will immediately run away.

If you're determined to make your ex-boyfriend suffer, the best way to accomplish this is to make him realise – I mean, *really* make him believe – that you don't miss him in the least and that there's absolutely *zero* chance that you will ever permit him to date you again. Committing revenge attacks may scare the crap out of him, but will cost you your dignity, make *you* look desperate, lonely and pathetic – not to mention insane. At the very worst, you might end up in prison or a mental hospital.

Never try to persuade a guy to give you another chance, unless he declares that you did something wrong, and that was the only reason for the split. If he indicates that he doesn't see long-term potential, trying to persuade him to reconcile with you will probably confuse him, and lead to a Gerard/Sarah-type scenario.

Chapter 9: Myths and Facts

A husband is living proof that a wife can take a joke.

There was a time when conventional scientific wisdom held that the female orgasm was a myth – not to mention *multiple* female orgasms. Personally, I'm inclined to take women at their word when it comes to orgasms – single or multiple – mostly because I like to pretend that none of my girlfriends ever faked an orgasm with me.

Anyway, this chapter is about the most persistent myths that women have about male behaviour and the male mind. Most of these myths were invented by filmmakers, television writers and comedians – and there's a little bit of truth to some of them. But when listening to some women, you'd think these myths were iron-clad facts, not humorous clichés. Here then, is my list of top myths/facts on the male mind.

Myth: ***Men are commitment phobes.***
Fact: ***It only seems that most men are commitment phobes***, because men often use this as an excuse for ditching women. In 90% of instances, men break up with women because they don't really fancy them, or when they aren't yet ready to settle down and get married. Men who aren't ready for marriage tend to be:

- *Young and inexperienced* when it comes to dating and relationships. Young men always think the grass is greener elsewhere. Until they've had experience with a number of women, they probably won't want a long-term relationship. Trying to convince a man who's had only one or two girlfriends before you that it's time to commit to something serious is like trying to convince him to attend an Oktoberfest in Munich, and limit himself to the first style of beer that he tastes. He may abide by your wishes, but he will wonder what the other varieties taste like – and eventually the desire to find out may overwhelm his good judgment.

- *Insecure about his career and/or finances.* When a man is focused on establishing his career, winning a promotion or salary raise, or especially if he's having problems related to jobs and money, he is unlikely to want to commit to marriage or a long-term relationship. Men like to get all their "ducks in a row" when it comes to career status and material success before they feel confident enough to worry about romantic relationships. Give him the time and space to sort out these issues, and if he's the right one for you, he'll come around.

- *Unwilling to accept responsibility for supporting a wife and children.* This usually harkens back to career and money issues. If not – if he's earning a comfortable living, well-established in his career and over 30 – this guy may actually fear commitment. On the other hand, maybe he doesn't want children. If he does want children and still won't commit, then you are probably dealing with a bona fide commitment-phobe.

Myth: **All men will cheat if given the opportunity.**

Fact: **Although most men flirt with other women** after they've entered committed relationships, they will only cheat if:

- *Something is seriously amiss in your relationship.* The potential list of what's amiss might include everything from your moribund love life to an after-the-fact discovery that you and he have almost nothing in common. The vast majority of men do *not* have sex with other women when they're happy and content in a relationship.

- *They are preparing to end your relationship/marriage.* If a man has mentally checked out of a relationship, he may get involved with another woman as a prelude to physically checking out. This is the equivalent of "purchasing an insurance policy" before going skydiving. Regardless of whether they are conscious of this or not, some men hedge their bets before calling things off with their girlfriends or wives. It's something they've learned from their careers – never quit your job before you've already landed a new one.

- *Exceptional circumstances arise.* This is a polite way of saying that some men will cheat when another woman makes it obvious that she wants to have a one-night stand, and he thinks there's almost no chance that you'll find out. The circumstances that most often lead to such a tryst involve the husband or boyfriend who travels frequently on business, and who usually stays in hotels with cocktail lounges. He encounters a beautiful woman at the bar, and she makes it obvious that she wants him – wants him back in her room. Now, the man is in a quandary. Although he believes in sexual fidelity, he's just been presented with the three key elements needed to induce "criminal behaviour" – means, motive and opportunity. Actually, he doesn't need a hell of a lot of motive, since his Cro-Magnon instincts and hormones inspire horniness whenever he spots an attractive female, but the fact that this woman is practically seducing him can sometimes prove irresistible. That said, many men will not succumb to such temptation. But I wouldn't be on it. Fortunately, exceptional circumstances are usually just that – exceptional (and rare).

Myth: *Men have one-track minds.*

Fact: *Sex is a major drive*, especially for young men with raging hormones. But it's far from the only thing men want from women. Once those hormones *do* take control, however, a man can become like a "Manchurian Candidate," seemingly brainwashed to pursue the singular goal of obtaining sex. This can induce a truly powerful case of male hyper-concentration and focus. That's why it's important that women try to slow things down, and not be available for sex too quickly. When horny, the male will do or say almost anything to get into bed with a woman. However, the moment he completes his orgasm, he will suddenly regain the capacity for rational thought. At that moment, he will know whether he actually fancies you or has made a terrible mistake.

I don't know what it feels like to be a woman, or how women feel after achieving orgasm. But as a man, I can tell you that testosterone is a very potent hormone – one that would probably be banned for men under the age of 25 if it weren't already coursing through their veins. The more sexually excited a man becomes, the less likely he is to behave logically. He's much less likely to care how or with whom he has sex.

Irrational behaviour during arousal was the subject of a study conducted at the University of California at Berkeley several years ago. The male (college-age) subjects were given a questionnaire to fill out during normal states and states of heightened sexual arousal. During non-aroused states, only a few men reported they would engage in immoral sexual behaviour, or that they were aroused by things like women's shoes or the thought of having sex with 60-year-old women. In a state of arousal, however, their answers tended to change.

Here's a random sampling of questions and answers from this study:

Question	Non-Aroused	Aroused
Are women's shoes erotic?	42%	65%
Can you imagine having sex with a 60-year-old woman?	7%	23%
Is it frustrating to do nothing more than just kiss?	41%	69%
Could you enjoy having sex with someone you hated?	53%	77%
Is birth control the woman's responsibility?	34%	44%[2]

I suppose it's accurate to say that men have one-track minds when they're in a state of arousal. Otherwise, it's safe to say that men normally have multi-track minds, and that arousal causes the different tracks to converge at a Grand Central Terminal of Lust.

2   Airely, Dan. Predictably Irrational. New York: HarperCollins, 2008.

Myth: Men can't take no for an answer.

Fact: Men take "no" for an answer all the time. Stalkers and psychopaths aside, the average man *does* take "no" for an answer. Of course, many will men push the envelope of acceptable foreplay with a new girlfriend – to see just how far they can get before hearing "no." In their minds (and groins) this is perfectly normal and instinctive behaviour. They expect that the average woman will let them remove only so much clothing or touch only certain body parts during their early make-out sessions. Then, once the man and woman have gotten to know each other well enough – and the man has proven that he's going to stick around for a little while – he expects to go "all the way" within a particular timeframe. Problems with "no" do happen, but usually when:

- People with incompatible values start dating – e.g., a woman who doesn't believe in premarital sex dates a man who *does* expect premarital sex.

- *Players* or Bad Boys are involved.

- The man and/or the woman get drunk.

Drink responsibly, my friends. When it comes to dating, mating and sex, the vast majority of problem situations are caused by alcohol and drugs.

Speaking of booze …

Myth: In vito veritus (In wine, there is truth).

Fact: This is very far from the truth. Alcohol is *not* a truth serum, and it's unfortunate that so many people believe this ancient myth, particularly women. Women often email me to complain that their boyfriends finally "confessed" their true feelings under the influence of alcohol, and they had to be unceremoniously dumped. Whilst some words and deeds are not easily (or ever) forgiven, that fifth glass of ale or that fourth martini was probably not the cause of his outburst. As I mentioned earlier, alcohol reduces your inhibitions, decreases your capacity for rational thought and – most important – magnifies your emotions out of all proportion.

A perfectly sober boyfriend might never complain about the mole on your chin, because it's not very important to him when it comes to your overall appearance. But when he pours enough booze down his throat, he might make an unflattering comment. He might even obsess over the mole. But that does not mean he's always obsessed over that little mole, and he suddenly can't stand to be seen in public with you. In fact, he might never have even consciously thought about the stupid mole until you raised the subject while he was inebriated. And chances are, he'll be very upset with himself the next morning for saying anything – if he even remembers what happened the night before.

The fact is, *nobody* can predict how he will behave if he's had too much to drink. By and large, people in my circles tend to laugh more and get overly sentimental. But some people – not just men – can become angry, aggressive and even violent under the influence of alcohol. People who normally display sunny dispositions might say and do things that remind you of a documentary on Nazi Germany. This doesn't mean that they are secret Nazis, any more than the normally gruff and angry barfly in the corner is a closet philosopher when he waxes poetic (after ten pints of ale).

In short, people don't behave like themselves when they drink too much, so don't give any credence to the idea that there is truth in wine.

By the way, I get a *lot* of emails from women whose descriptions of their boyfriends make it clear that these men are alcoholics. If your husband or boyfriend drinks regularly and excessively, do a little online research to determine if he has a problem and needs help. Alcoholism is *much* a more common problem than you might think, since most cases go undiagnosed and untreated.

Myth: *Making him jealous will win his loyalty.*

Fact: *Bad idea.* Men do *not* like to be made jealous. If you attempt to make a man jealous by flirting with other men, or suggesting that other men are more attractive/successful/wealthy, etc., watch out! You have just opened a Pandora's Box. There's a good chance that your boyfriend will become irate, start an argument or even start a fist fight with the man you're pretending to like. He may even dump you on the spot and immediately search for another girlfriend – and probably not in that order.

The typical male is so averse to being made jealous that he will get angry even when he *knows* that you're just feigning interest in another man.

Why?

For one thing, men hate being the pawns in women's mind games. For another, men are competitive by nature, so even when he's consciously aware that you're just trying to get a rise out of him, he won't be able to shut off his instincts. The Cro-Magnon side of his brain will want to tear apart any rival who dares tempt you into his cave. Therefore, playing the jealousy card is a bit like teasing a caged lion – with the door to the cage wide open.

Keep in mind, however, that men don't mind when a *woman* displays a little jealousy herself. As I mentioned earlier, men like it when a woman gently teases or chastises him about his wandering eye, which gives him the opportunity to demonstrate his love and loyalty. Yes, this is a double standard, but I wouldn't advise trying to change it – unless you enjoy real-life drama, not to mention spending weekends by yourself.

It's in man's nature to try to convince as many women as possible that he is desirable – whether or not he intends to do anything about it. This doesn't stop when he's dating a woman, if he's in a relationship with a woman, or when he's married. Try to forget that he sometimes flirts with other women, knowing that *you* are the one he takes home at the end of the day. There's no point in getting jealous if he gawks at another woman. There are millions of woman in the world, and he'd have to be blind not to stare at most of them and flirt with some of them. It's in his nature.

Myth: **Men want women with really big breasts.**
Fact: **Men notice women with big breasts, but tastes vary.** When it comes to a woman's boobs, men have individual preferences. In addition, tastes vary by culture, and trends wax and wane over time. During the Elizabethan Age, for example, the ideal woman had a bra size of roughly 34-C. Raleigh, Shakespeare and Marlowe preferred lusty ladies with firm, orange-sized breasts. Women with especially *large* breasts were considered less attractive, except as nursemaids.

Myth: **Men lie more than women.**
Fact: **Women lie just as often as men.** I'm amazed at how often women question my veracity. For some reason, women automatically presume I'm lying when I say just about anything. Maybe it's my face. In my experience, however, women lie as often as men, and probably

more. The difference is that women characterize their dishonesty as "white lies," whereas men turn red-faced and deny it.

Because women lie so much, they assume that men lie just as much. Therefore, women often read too much into what a guy says, and pass every sentence through a mental polygraph in search of inconsistencies. Between their mental lie detector and the fact that they usually remember every syllable a man has uttered, they often "catch" men in inconsistencies, which they define as lies. For example, if a man tries to rephrase a statement so it more accurately reflects his thoughts, women shout "Ah ha!" and point to this as an example of a lie. Hence, women "catch" men lying all the time, because they are always looking for lies. Meanwhile, men don't really care about small lies and exaggerations.

It's true that men often brag or exaggerate, sometimes inflating the truth. However, these are mere embellishments, since there is always a kernel of truth to the story. Men feel the need to hype their lives because women's lives seem far more interesting and exciting. Indeed, men often exaggerate stories with their friends. A favourite male pastime spending hour after hour in pubs, trading hyperbolic stories with friends and strangers alike. And I can tell you this: these friends and strangers would *never* dare to question the veracity of the stories, no matter how ridiculous they were.

Myth: **Men in happy relationships have no interest in porn.**
Fact: **Only dead men have no interest in porn.**

Chapter 10: Troubleshooting Guide

A woman says to her friend, "My husband's an angel."
The other replies, "You're lucky. Mine's still alive."

Some of the questions I receive from female readers didn't fit elsewhere in the book, so I've added them here in the form of FAQs.

Q: *If I get into a romantic relationship with my best friend, and things don't work out, will the friendship be ruined?*

A: Probably. And that's because friends set lower standards for each other. First, they needn't be physically attracted or sexually compatible. Second, romantic partners share more time and emotional intimacy than best friends usually do. You'll see a side of your friend that you never knew existed, and this isn't always good. Even if you two decide to have an amicable parting, the negative thoughts and behaviour you witnessed during the romance will stick with you. Then, there's the embarrassment factor that occurs if you discover that you're not sexually compatible, especially if one partner turns out to be a rotten lover. The partner who blames himself for the problems (and this *will* happen) will probably resent the other person, or he'll be afraid that you'll tell everyone he's a terrible lover.

Even if you manage to stay friendly afterward, things won't be the same. On the other hand, if you merely want to have sex with a friend to see what it would be like, *that* doesn't always destroy a friendship. I've known a number of friends who had one-night stands out of sexual curiosity, and remained good friends afterward. But these people established clear "just-this once" ground rules in advance.

Q: *Is it possible to spot a Player or a stalker right away?*

A: Yes. *The Player* is easy to identify, as he'll be alternately greeted and insulted by every woman you pass on the street. He will probably own a boxed DVD set of *The Pick-Up Artist*, as well as books on the subject, and have a fully stocked liquor cabinet. A potential *Stalker* is also easy to spot – if you know what to look for. He has awkward social skills (or none at all), and will begin referring to you as his "girlfriend" shortly before or after the first date – or even shortly after you acknowledge his existence. He may also shower you with inappropriate or outrageously expensive gifts from the get-go. Your best defence is prevention. Take a cue from the men, here, and disappear as fast as you can. Any attempts to let him down gently will backfire, as only his previous stalking victims have ever shown the least bit of kindness to him. Basically, he falls obsessively in love with any woman who'll give him the time of day.

Q: *What's the best way to finish things with a man?*

A: Gently, but firmly. Tell him you want to end the relationship and *why*. Think of a nice way to express your feelings, but be honest. If a man fancies you, and doesn't want things to end, he will insist that he can change and (since men are natural problem-solvers) will quickly explain how this remarkable change will be accomplished. Do not leave the door open to the slightest possibility of reconciliation. If you do, he will sneak through that crack, and it will be the devil to get rid of him.

Q: *WHEN is the best time to finish things with a man?*

A: If you mean what time of day and what venue, I suggest daytime and a public setting – in case he takes things *REALLY* badly. If you mean, "At what point in the relationship should I realize that this guy isn't Mr. Right," that depends on your age and experience. As a rule, it's time to break up when you'd rather stay home than see him again. If you have a lot of dating experience and you're over 18, don't waste your time on casual relationships. Every relationship should be serious, or at least a learning experience. Even if it doesn't last, use discipline to get out of a relationship if it's not right, because the clock is ticking. The longer you stay in that relationship, the longer it will take for you to find the right guy. You have to meet the wrong guys before you meet the right guy – that's another rule. The longer it takes for you to get over a bad guy, the more likely you will not see a decent guy staring you straight in the face. You are too busy crying about the guy you gave 10 chances, you've probably ignored the 10 Mr. Rights who just crossed your path.

Q: *When should I mention that I'm a single mom?*

A: As soon as it's obvious that a man fancies you. If you're dealing with a man who's willing to date a single mother, this news shouldn't affect your chances for a relationship. If you're dealing with a man who *doesn't* want to get involved with a woman *and* her child (or children), he will opt out before you've invested too much time and energy. It's best to give him the facts upfront. That said, you don't have to blurt out, "I've got a kid" the moment he asks what time it is.

Q: *When a man says he wants to keep the relationship casual because he's just coming off a bad relationship, does he just want sex?*

A: Yes. Maybe he *is* coming off a bad relationship. So what? If he's not ready to commit to marriage or living together, that's one thing. That's not the same as wanting a "casual relationship," which is a code for "fooling around." If you push a man into making a commitment before he's ready, he may ask you to slow down. But he won't tell you that all he wants is a casual relationship. No relationship involving sex – especially from a woman's viewpoint – is ever completely casual. If he likes you enough to have sex, but not enough to *eventually* commit or consider the possibility of committing in the future, he knows that things aren't going to work out, but he wants to keep having sex for a while.

Q: *He never takes me where I want to go. Or he always wants to just stay home. What can I do?*

A: Women tend to hold back instead of offering suggestions on where to go and what to do. This is problematic, because most men have no idea where to go and what to do. Therefore, if you'd like to visit the seaside tomorrow, don't hassle him until he says yes. Just let him know you're interested in that. And don't be too subtle. Many men have no imagination when it comes to deciding where to take a woman. Some men prefer women to help them make the decisions by offering clues, but the clues must be obvious. Remember, men don't do subtle. Tip: Never hint that you hate the place he's just taken you, because you'll make him feel guilty and foolish. Women are usually much better at planning holidays and social outings, and he probably wants to use those talents. He won't want you to hold back and say "whatever" when he makes a lame suggestion. There's nothing worse than when a woman won't contribute ideas, and then spends the outing with a sullen frown on her face.

Q: *I'm shy, but so is the man I fancy. What should I do?*

A: If you both stand there and do nothing, you'll never build a relationship. The only way to solve this problem is for one (or both of you) to take a chance, and ask the other person out. I know it's difficult, but you must force yourself to overcome your fear of rejection for at least one brief, shining moment. Nothing ventured, nothing gained.

Q: *I'm over 40. Is it too late for marriage or a serious relationship?*

A: Absolutely not. Though most men don't date women who are significantly older, and actually prefer women who are younger, there are many tactics you can use to increase your odds. For one thing, looks matter more to men that actual chronological age. If you're 45, but you look 18, you're "problem" is solved – even after you drop the bombshell that you're over 40. The only time age matters much these days are when it comes to Internet dating. In theory, men will search for younger women, and sometimes your photos may not be a good indicator of how young and vibrant you look in real life. So you may want to keep your age a secret until you've had a chance to meet the man in person. Then, of course, there's the obvious solution of dating a man closer to your own age – or even older.

Q: *What if I have stretch marks, or a spot on my butt, or …?*

A: Please! If he's attracted to you physically or otherwise, he won't even notice the stretch marks or the spot on your butt, etc. – much less care about it. It's not as though *he* doesn't have any flaws, right?

Q: *Won't he think I'm boring and that my life is boring?*

A: He's probably thinking the exact same thing about himself. When a man really fancies a woman, and isn't just hoping for a quickie, he sees the woman as a princess. As I mentioned in Chapter 1, he is literally unable to detect any physical flaws, and simply adores both her looks and personality. She basically becomes a superstar in his eyes. Keep in mind that life is not like a movie or soap opera – or any other fantasy world invented by creative minds. Bruce Willis doesn't really go around shooting people, getting beaten up for 30 minutes and then walking away without a scratch, and saving damsels in distress. He wakes up in the morning like everyone else, goes to the toilet and has something to eat. He's only human, and probably had the same concerns about seeming too boring when he was dating.

Q: *No man will date me because I'm fat, right?*

A: It's true that if you are really fat – and I mean *obese* (not "I'm so fat and waiting for him to tell me that I'm thin"), then the worldwide pool of interested suitors will be substantially reduced. In that case, you can lose weight to increase the number of guys who might fancy you, or look for men who appreciate voluptuous women. Overall, men like women of various shapes and sizes. It's true that the ideal female has a 7-10 waist-to-hip ratio, but this doesn't mean that *some* men don't find other shapes attractive. In addition, you don't have to be thin to have a 7-10 waist-to-hip ratio. If you have wider hips, you can still maintain a ratio of 0.7 if your waist is still 70% of the circumference of your hips. As for women who pretend they are fat – who just had a bar of chocolate and can *see* those extra pounds in the mirror – stop being silly. If you were to ask men which woman they find more attractive, stick thin Kate Moss or the curvier faced Mylene Klass, the vast majority would choose Mylene Klass.

Q: *I'm told that men like dumb girls. Should I pretend to be ditzy to avoid scaring men away?*

A: Dumb men like dumb girls. Intelligent men sometimes *pretend* to like dumb girls to get them in bed. But in general, men prefer to be with women who are roughly as intelligent and educated as themselves. Feel free to wear a big button that displays your tremendously high IQ.

Q: *Since "absence makes the heart grow fonder," should I take a 10-day Caribbean cruise to recapture my boyfriend's waning interest in me?*

A: I wouldn't risk it. Your absence may only make his heart fonder for the woman sitting nearest him in the local pub. If you're already in a long-term relationship, your absence may increase his longing, but if the relationship is pretty new, he might use your absence to have a fling with someone else. You'd better take him along on that cruise.

Q: *I'm still a virgin, and a little scared of sex. Will a man hold my lack of experience against me, or do men prefer virgins?*

A: Before losing their virginity, men are also terrified of sex. Actually, they are mostly terrified of being such crappy lovers that the woman will laugh in their faces. As for preferring virgins, most of the men I've known would rather be with a woman who has *some* sexual experience – e.g., who knows where to find the man's parts and knows what to do with them – but they don't want a woman who slept with every guy in her college dormitory. Some religious types insist that their women be virgins on their wedding nights, but that's another story.

Q: *I'm worried that I'm so attractive that I scare men away. What can I do without making myself ugly?*

A: First, get over yourself – nobody's *that* beautiful. Second, though some men will be intimated by a woman's good looks, thinking they're out of her league, their behaviour has less to do with her objective gorgeousness than their individual tolerance for rejection. A self-confident Alpha Man will never find *any* woman too beautiful to approach. But someone with the self-esteem of a troll would be intimidated by a woman whose face resembled a carved pumpkin. Men like beauty. Hate rejection. By way of proof, consider the rare woman who is beautiful *and* approachable. These women are routinely mobbed by swarms of horny men.

Q: *Should I offer to split the bill for dinner? Or will a man be insulted by this?*

A: It doesn't hurt to offer to split the bill. Most guys prefer to pay for the initial dates. A few prefer to pay forever. These days, men know that women often work and earn money, too. Even so, most don't mind paying the bills for a while. They just don't want to feel that they're being used for free food and entertainment. A guy usually negotiates this delicate territory without causing an argument. If you offer to pay, he will flatly refuse, accept, or offer to split the bill. If the topic causes arguments or enough discomfort to break up the relationship, I'd argue that the relationship was doomed from the start. Therefore, you should look forward to the arrival of the check as a way of testing whether the relationship will work. View it as a litmus test instead of a stumbling block.

Q: *My boyfriend never shows up for dates on time (and sometimes he doesn't show up at all, and makes lame excuses). What should I do?*

A: This behaviour displays a lack of respect for you and your feelings. Even if the habitual tardiness is the result of a genetic trait (see "Explorer" in Chapter 7), there's no valid excuse for continually arriving late, or not arriving at all, for something as important as a date. When men do this, I'm inclined to believe that they're not really that interested in the woman – unless they have a job that often demands that they work late or be available at a moment's notice – doctors, policemen, firemen, lawyers, etc. (Self-employed men often keep odd hours, but this doesn't count since these men are their *own* bosses.) My advice is to honestly explain how you feel about his tardiness and/or "no-shows." If this doesn't solve the problem, dump his ass. He's probably not that "into' you if he doesn't respond to a gentle warning. Whatever you do, resist the temptation to retaliate by showing up late yourself. In addition to the fact that "two wrongs don't make a right," this will only cause things to escalate. I had two friends who worked near each other, and used to schedule a regular lunch meeting for Thursdays. But one guy always showed up at least 15 minutes late, so his friend retaliated by showing up 15 minutes late himself. The first time that Friend #1 had to wait a few minutes for the normally on-time guy to arrive, it started a war. Each friend showed up later and later, so as not to be the one standing on the street for any length of time. Eventually, the situation got so out of control that they had to cancel the lunches. By the way, neither of them ever said a word about the other being late. The whole war was undeclared.

www.ingramcontent.com/pod-product-compliance
Lightning Source LLC
Chambersburg PA
CBHW030346290526
45785CB00004B/1618